THE OUTDOOR IDEA BOOK

Illustrated by artistic contributors
and by
WENDY WALLIN

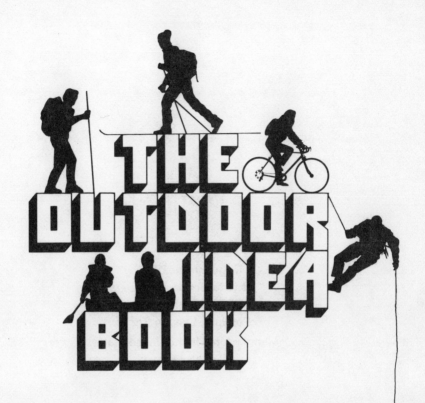

THE OUTDOOR IDEA BOOK

Collected and Edited by
JUNE FLEMING

Victoria House   Portland, Oregon

Library of Congress Cataloging in Publication Data
Main entry under title:

The Outdoor idea book.

  Bibliography: p.
  Includes index.
  1. Outdoor recreation—United States. 2. Outdoor
recreation—Canada. 3. Outdoor life. I. Fleming June.
GV191.4.086   796.5′0973   78-6514
ISBN 0-918480-06-X

Contents

Also by June Fleming:
The Well-Fed Backpacker

THE OUTDOOR IDEA BOOK

And now,
a word from your editor . . .

"Thank You!"

    This book had many creators . . . hundreds of individuals, organizations and publications had a direct or indirect hand in making it happen. They *all* deserve our most enthusiastic thanks, since it couldn't have happened without their co-operation and sharing.

THANK YOU to those who helped spread the word, verbally and in print, that we wanted to receive ideas for the book. They thought enough of the notion to endorse it by passing on our request for contributions, thus enabling us to reach thousands more individuals than would otherwise have been possible.

    Dozens of newspapers and magazines throughout the United States and Canada were supplied with information on the project, but we have no way of saying thank you to *all* who printed it, since we can't know who they are. Many contributors to the book cited where they read about it, and so we're pleased to be able to thank *Wilderness Camping* magazine, *Backpacking Journal, Summit* magazine, and *Mother Earth News.* We wish we could name them all.

    We also sent information to outdoor organizations all over North America and were very pleased at their willingness to let members know (through announcements at meetings and in newsletters) that we needed their help . . . Sierra Club chapters, the Adirondack Forty-Sixers, Florida Trail Association, Appalachian Mountain Club chapters, and many, many more. Once again, our frustration is not knowing every single one.

Word of the project was also sent to hundreds of individuals around the country, with a request that they share it with outdoor organizations they are part of, or with local newspapers. Since suggestions were received from all but a few states and from most parts of Canada, we assume that our plea for contributions was printed many times over, and only wish we knew *exactly* who to thank!

THANK YOU to those individuals who shared their ideas. Often quite a bit of time and effort was invested to describe a procedure or piece of gear, and perhaps illustrate it with a sketch. Many envelopes were lumpy with illustrations, examples, mini-models of homemade gear, samples of a packaging technique. Checking the post office box provided a steady stream of excitement, as contributions came from all over. Frequently there were delightful letters full of the enthusiasm which marks creative, outdoor-oriented souls. I tried out many of the ideas—either to get a clearer understanding of how they worked, test their practicality, or simply because they sounded like a lot of fun!

Contributors range in age from teens to seniors, in experience from beginner to seasoned trekker, in habit from solitary to gregarious, in terrain preference from desert to snowfield. The common link of which many spoke and which all obviously share is a deep love of wild places. I wish it had been possible to reply individually to each person who so generously shared of his/her own learning and experience . . . but I'll do it collectively here. The names of those whose suggestions were chosen appear in the book. Appreciation also goes to those whose ideas, for one reason or another, don't appear. Their sharing was sincere and freely given, and so is our gratitude.

June Fleming

Introduction

This is a book written by people who are out *doing* things in the wilderness . . . people who thrive on zesty, basically self-propelled activities such as hiking, backpacking, canoeing, bicycling, climbing, snowshoeing, cross-country skiing, snow camping. All these activities put a person in very direct, challenging, invigorating contact with his environment and call for an ability to adapt, be resourceful and sturdy, find satisfaction in solving problems with a maximum of ingenuity and a minimum of external technological help. In fact, one of the chief delights of engaging in self-propelled pastimes is that of coming up with new ideas and then sharing them with kindred souls.

It is a natural wilderness lover's urge to be always on the lookout for new ideas: a nifty piece of homemade gear; a friend's different approach to solving our universal need for lightweight, multi-use equipment; a better way to travel, cook, sleep, make a backpack more functional; deal with the weather or critters or terrain. One person simply can't think of everything himself! So he keeps an eager ear cocked for those gems he might have thought of himself, but didn't. Each nugget of shared wisdom we gain from another wilderness person, whether a close friend or a stranger we meet briefly on the trail, becomes a real prize, part of us and all our future outdoor experiences, probably passed on again and again in that great perpetual community learning cycle. Wouldn't it be a fine thing if somehow we could spread ourselves abroad in the land to cover rivers, mountains and trails all over? Go to areas beyond the scope of what our personal time and mobility allow? Then we could exchange ideas with hundreds of others who love to be out in the wilds, and we'd *all* be better off!

That is what this book is all about: bringing together ideas shared by people throughout the United States and Canada—flashes of inspiration, hard-wrought solutions, ideas they have hit upon in the course of many miles logged on the rivers and trails of North America, of countless days and nights lived closely with the land. We asked folks from all over to share the bits of learning that have made their wilderness experiences more fun, comfortable, safe, efficient. We knew there was much creative thinking going on out there and felt a need to draw as much of it as possible together into one pot—a zesty, bubbling stew, if you will, of rich, hearty, useful ingredients to feed and warm us all! Our feeling that such a concoction is needed was reinforced time and again by those who submitted ideas. They were excited about the notion, wished us well, said such a book would be a service to many, and were delighted at the chance to be part of it.

The Outdoor Idea Book does not purport to be a comprehensive book of fundamentals for beginners. You won't find much discussion of sleeping-bag construction, or how to use a map and compass, meet medical emergencies in the woods, or buy a tent. These things are all necessary matters to be given serious consideration by everyone who ventures away from civilization, but they are well-treated elsewhere and lie outside the scope of this book.

Once a person gets actively involved in things self-propelled, he has probably acquired the basic equipment needed—sleeping bag, pack, stove, boots, etc.—and a certain minimal fund of skills and knowledge about how to use these things to help him get around in the wilds. In the basic learning stages of his engagement with the wilderness, he can go to many fine resource books and perhaps take a class or two at his community college, park bureau, or YMCA. If he wants to purchase some major piece of equipment, such as a tent, boots, sleeping bag, he can find ample discussion in many books of the options available so he can weigh the pros and cons before making the decision that fits him best. For those who may be interested, a list of some of the most helpful books providing such basic information is given at the end of this book.

Our aim with *The Outdoor Idea Book* is to go a much-needed step beyond these resources and make available a shared fund of knowledge from a broad representation of the doers who have continued to learn happy coexistence with the wilds. The notions gathered here represent the next layer up from the bare basics. They are adaptations, expansions, and refinements built on good solid foundations of knowledge and equipment. Here are answers to such questions as: Is there a *better* way to use this gear? Is there a piece of equipment I can make to solve this problem? How can I package food to save more space and be handier to prepare? Is it possible to keep things *really* dry in a storm?

It is the inherent nature of wilderness experience that there is no end to the learning. No matter whether you've been out twice, twenty or a thousand times, you will never see the trail sign that says, "You have arrived—you have learned all you need to know." And thank goodness! That learning is a large part of the joy we find in being out there.

Two special characteristics distinguish this book((1) Its contents are the shared ideas of hundreds of wilderness lovers, individual people with their own styles of discovering, doing things and telling about them; (2) The ideas come from all over North America rather than just one region, and should therefore be helpful to folks who do their adventuring on the Appalachian Trail, a Minnesota lake, the plains of the Midwest, or the high country of California, Alberta, or Colorado.

Most of the suggestions are presented here in their original form, using the words of their creators. You will have the added pleasure of meeting a new friend, as he would talk with you should you chance to meet on a trail in his part of the country. Often contributors told their ideas in the context of a little information about who they are, where they usually do their wandering, with perhaps a slice of some wilderness experience. We did a bit of editing in the interest of clarity, but we didn't attempt to rewrite all the submissions into a smoothly flowing, uniform style. That might have been somewhat easier to read, but it would also have watered down the flavor of diversity and individuality which we prize about this collection. More than a smoothly readable work, we valued producing a usable compilation true to its beginnings—informal grammar and all. This is, after all, not a novel but a resource book!

Some of the sketches that accompanied contributions are used here just as they were originally drawn, some were touched up a little, and some provided the springboard for illustrations that give a little broader treatment to the ideas.

We felt readers and users of the book would be interested in knowing who contributed each ideas and where he lives. A credit line therefore appears with each suggestion (with the exception of those coming from the editor's experiences or knowledge, or that of her family).

Please Read This Part

A word about the contents and organization of the book. As news of the project got around and we began receiving contributions from folks all over, many of their suggestions fell naturally into several very large and basic categories, such as information having to do with packs, homemade gear, sleeping, cooking. Others were dandy, useful ideas concerning an area not so broad and general—traveling with small children, dealing with very cold weather, aids for canoeists. Dozens of the hints shared apply to more than one phase of outdoor experience. For example: a plastic water bottle can be a container for mixing drinks or pudding, a hot water bottle to warm your toes when tucked into the foot of your sleeping bag, or a means of thawing frozen boots in the morning. And a given idea may have appeal for several different reasons: perhaps it suggests a way to pare equipment down to the least possible bulk or weight; it may have special benefits to a person traveling long distances or alone; maybe it costs very little or makes use of recyclable items already on hand; perhaps it sparks the self-reliant, creative part of one who enjoys making his own gear.

All these factors told us that a thorough system of *cross-referencing* must help structure the book. It is meant to be *used*, and will be read by people who probably have specific reasons for wanting to enhance their wilderness experiences (like saving money or weight, expanding their food horizons, or building competence to venture into newer, more difficult terrain). That is why each idea will be fully explained (and sometimes illustrated, for clarity) in one section where it most obviously fits, and then referred to in perhaps two or three other sections. The index should aid further in the search for answers to a reader's specific questions.

The substance of *The Outdoor Idea Book* ranges far and wide, from the planning and home preparation phases of excursions, to things that will help you preserve and recall them when they are past. In between you'll find dozens of detailed suggestions on making a trek comfortable and safe; finding, collecting and carrying water; discouraging the encroachment of flying and walking critters; keeping your feet warm and your pillow quiet at night; using a garbage bag a dozen ways; making useful items such as a tent, a combination tarp and signaling device, or a pair of rain pants; recycling innumerable containers and other items for use in the outback; lighting a fire under adverse conditions; packing gear in ways that organize and protect it; setting up camp in the snow; keeping your camera easily accessible while hiking; modifying clothes to do the job you need while cutting weight and bulk; planning and packaging foods for gourmet eating on the trail; setting up an enjoyable and ecologically sound camp.

So here you have a potpourri of ideas for wilderness lovers, meant to make those fine times even finer. There are hundreds presented, and our hope is that among them each of you will find at least a few dozen that spark your particular fancy and make your own adventures just that much more pleasurable.

Part I
At-Home Planning and Preparation

At-Home Planning and Preparation

When a trek to the wilds is born in your mind—at your desk, over a beer with good friends, or while wistfully daydreaming on a rainy, confining evening—it has in fact already begun. You find yourself planning an itinerary, checking out your gear and clothing, drawing up menus.

You may be one of those who enjoy making advance preparations all the time, whether or not a definite trip is on the calendar. If so, when you come across an interesting recipe for trail snacks you make up a big batch and freeze them in trail-size portions, ready to pack when an adventure crystallizes. A file folder collects articles and ideas gathered from magazines and friends. On the lookout for gear you can make yourself, you may be just waiting to try out those snazzy rain chaps or the new lightweight shelter you whipped up on an idle evening last month. Once or twice a year a batch of firestarters is readied. And whenever a tidy, lightweight container of some sort passes through your household, you pounce on it after it's empty (sometimes even before) and transform it for a whole new function outdoors!

Those of us who find our most *real* days are the ones spent on a trail, river, or in a snow-clad wood know that this part of our lives is not an isolated escape or respite from reality. Instead, it permeates all our days and infuses them with a quality of delicious anticipation. While our bodies appear to be going about their usual city-business, our hearts are really in the hills . . . and anything we can do to keep the transition paths open and in good repair is done!

1.

Making Your Backpack and Its Contents More Serviceable

No matter how simple or elaborate your pack is to start with, there are many ways to extend the range of what it can do for you and strengthen the teamwork between you and your pack. Some of the suggested modifications are as simple as a five-cent clipped-on addition. Others require a slightly larger investment of money and some tinkering time. How you organize gear and load it into your pack has a lot to do with its serviceability, and several suggestions deal with this. Also shared are hints concerning map care, repairs to packs and other equipment, and personal care gear.

Once you develop a system of organization that works for you, stick to it and continue to carry things in the same places so they can be readily located. And the more items you can simply store in your pack between trips, the fewer things you'll forget and the quicker you can hit the trail! The expense of a second toothbrush that always stays packed is well worth it!

STRIPS FOR SAFETY

While driving through the White Mountain National Forest one evening, returning from a long weekend trek, I passed several other hikers walking by the roadside. Today's backpacks are made in "plastic colors," but these reds, oranges, etc., do not show up at night, as became evident to me then. The consequences of this could be fatal to a person wearing a cumbersome pack on a curving remote road approached by an automobile driver who neither expects nor sees this pedestrian.

As soon as I discovered the problem, I knew the solution. I am also involved in emergency work and saw that the reflective cloth firemen have on their turnout coats was just the answer. These reflective strips can be either sewn or ironed on the back of a pack. The 3M Company makes this material and it is also available from local suppliers to firemen.

Friends and I ironed two 3-inch strips on to the back of our packs, and the result was very dramatic when illuminated by car headlights at night. I tested it and discovered that even on an easy curve, the hiker is made gradually more visible to the driver. On a straightaway, even at long distances, the strips almost light up.

An unexpected benefit was learned when returning to the lean-to one evening from a short side trip. Our flashlights caught the reflective strips of our packs leaning against the shelter, homing us in. I now place my pack accordingly when a similar situation is anticipated. It is not hard to see that in an emergency this little feature could prove invaluable.

H. Robert Yeager, Millis, MA

WHO BELONGS TO THIS?

Some items are not easily identified by the owner when a community clean-up takes place. One way to help in holding on to your spoon, cup or pot that looks like everyone else's is to mark your gear with nail polish using your initials, special logo or some similar means to identify your small equipment. Use of an outlandish color helps start evening conversations. Larger gear should be better marked than as mentioned above. Simply paint your equipment with a ''loud'' color such as orange, keeping in mind the intended use of each item being marked. For instance, you wouldn't want to use white paint on your snow stakes.

Thomas M. Minchin, Brooklyn, NY

MAKE YOUR PACK INDEPENDENT!

Finding a place to stand my pack was always a problem. So I attached two strips of lightweight metal extrusion to the top two clevis pins on my pack (wooden dowels will also work). Rubber chair leg tips may be added to the ends to avoid possible damage to your tent floor or groundcloth. Nylon cord or even old shoelaces hold the strips to the sides of the frame when not in use. The extra weight is minimal compared to the convenience.   *Ed Chevalier, Sidney, IL*

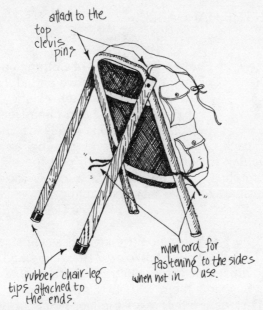

attach to the top clevis pins

rubber chair-leg tips attached to the ends.

nylon cord for fastening to the sides when not in use.

NON-SKID LOADING

Whenever I used to load my pack at home, I always had the problem of the plastic caps (plugging the bottom of the tubular frame) sliding on the floor away from the wall, and the pack falling. To end the problem, I purchased two rubber chair leg caps (15 cents each at variety and hardware stores) and slid them over the ends of the frame legs. No more slipping, and they pull off easily when you are ready to go. (Be sure to measure the diameter of your frame tubing, since these caps come in different sizes.)

Mark R. Koper, Wyoming, MI

STREAMLINE YOUR WALLET

A waterproof, non-bulky and almost weightless wallet is a small ziplock bag (available for pennies at outdoor stores) containing only the essentials: your driver's license, enough money for expenses to and from the trailhead, gasoline credit card, car and house keys.

SOME OF THE HANGABLES

For hanging articles of clothing on the back of my pack, I use two-ended clips I've made from a piece of elastic and two suspender clips. I hang mine from the top flap of my pack. One end is attached to the pack, and the other end can be attached to anything which is not so heavy it will pull the clip off the pack. These clips make an ideal place to dry socks as you walk! They also keep a jacket close at hand.

Wayne Geiser, Milford, NJ

Frustrated by tying line about your socks whilst attaching them to the back of your pack to dry? Buy four small alligator clips (used for electrical wiring connections). Suspend them with two small lengths of nylon line from D-rings or other available loops on your pack. Clip your socks in them to dry; you'll save time and never lose another sock! *Peter A. DeFazio, Eugene, OR*

A shower curtain hook is a wonderful, handy attachment for drying socks, bandanas, etc., for a loop-topped water bottle, or anything attachable to the back of a pack.

Charlene Priolo, Portland, OR

A 2¼-inch mini-carabiner can be used, too, although it is a little heavier.

The fishing supply department has safety snap swivels (about four for 39 cents) that are dandy for hanging water bottles and such from the outside of your pack. A cord or wire around the neck of the bottle goes through the loop on the swivel part, and the pin part hooks through a zipper pull tab, D-ring, or other suitable part of your pack.

Attach a few safety pins on the ring of your pocket knife.
Lorraine Kapakjian, Tenafly, NJ

A couple of climbing carabiners attached to the outside of your pack (through the leather patches that are on most packs, or any of the various loops or D-rings) are handy for securing many items to your pack. They have other uses, such as attaching to the end of a rope you need to throw over a limb. I use them to secure a 5-quart army surplus bladder canteen when traveling in dry country.
Robert W. Love, Whitmore Lake, MI

SILVER SUPERTAPE

Wrap a yard of duct tape (the 2-inch-wide silver tape sold in big rolls at most variety, hardware, and paper goods stores) around the frame of your pack in a spot where it won't rub against the pack or your body. This strong, waterproof tape which sticks to anything can be used in many emergency situations—to mend a rip in a sleeping bag, tent or plastic sack, patch a pair of pants, rain parka or other clothing, or even hold a boot together! It could even substitute for moleskin or tape a sprained ankle (remove from skin with TLC—remember, this was an *emergency*).
Pauli Budd, Richland, WA

HANDY CLEVIS PIN STORAGE

Instead of keeping extra clevis pins wrapped in a stuff sack or some pocket, I just fit them right on the D-ring loop of the pack wire (usually two pins). It can be done on any pack with clevis attachments; I've been using this method on a Kelty. Handy not to have to dig for a pin when you're pluggin' along! *Jim Pease, Burlington, VT*

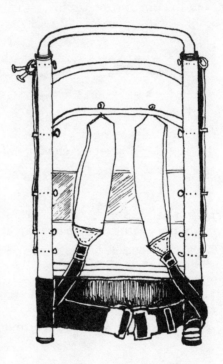

TACKLING A TOGGLE

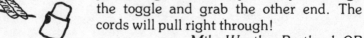

When threading two cords through a spring toggle, stick a pin through the ends, put the pin through the toggle and grab the other end. The cords will pull right through!

Mike Westby, Portland, OR

DRINKS FOR THE DAY

If your day pack doesn't have a handy place to store a water bottle, sew a pocket on the outside yourself.

CACHE AND CARRY

Pack, organize, cache and suspend your entire food supply in one pack that can be attached to your backpack. This is a large, strong stuff sack with zipper down one side and D-rings for attaching the sack to a pack or for suspending the whole thing from a high limb. Make it yourself or buy the one made by Trailhead CA). Use of such a bag keeps food, utensils, pots, etc. in one place; saves soiling your other stuff bags, avoids loss of small items. Pack it inside your pack or fasten to the top. Makes the whole cooking and eating operation simple, neat and easy; saves your food supply from the critters. Caching is now *required* in many areas. *Carol Lloyd, Oakland, CA*

PAD YOUR PACK AND YOUR SEAT

Use a piece of closed-cell foam pad inside your day pack to protect your back from the pokes of stray gear in the pack while hiking, and pull pad out at lunch time for a convenient "seat" to protect from the damp, chill ground.
Thomas M. Minchin, Brooklyn, NY

PACK-HANDLING EASE

To make pack-handling easier, tie a loose loop of lightweight rope around a few vertical and horizontal supports of the pack frame. It's an easy handle to grab and saves wear and tear on the pack and shoulder straps. It can also be used to hang up the pack at night.
Ed and Claire Weiser, Villa Park, IL

STRAP GUIDES

Sew two 2-inch-long pieces of webbing onto your sleeping bag stuff sack and slide the straps with which you lash the sack to your pack frame through them. This prevents the straps from slipping off the ends of the stuff sack.
Robert Burrell, Jr., Paonia, CO

SHOULDER STRAPS LAST LONGER

A short piece (1½ inches or so) of nylon webbing with a grommet in the center is used as a washer between a clevis-pin-mounted shoulder strap and the pack frame. This webbing takes the friction between the strap and the frame, thus prolonging the life of the shoulder strap or pad at the grommet, one of the first points to fail in normal use.

Chris Kounkel, Spokane, WA

YOU CAN TELL A ZIPPER BY ITS FOB

I collect key rings with anything interesting dangling from them, and attach them to the zipper tabs on my pack. The key fobs make finding and pulling the zipper much easier. In the dark, I know *exactly* which compartment I'm at, simply by the feel of each different key fob. They make interesting conversation pieces also. *Ed Chevalier, Sidney, IL*

SAFETY FIRST

Attach large, sturdy safety pins to the zipper tabs of your pack. They make managing zippers easier with gloved hands, provide a convenient way to hang light things from the pack, and can be removed and used in place of bulkier clothespins for hanging towels and clothes on limbs to dry (ever lost a washcloth to the breeze?).

EMERGENCY THREAD

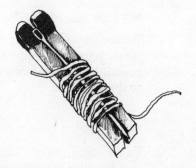

Wind dental floss around a needle slipped between two matches, carry in a secure place such as your first aid kit. It will sew up a rip in many kinds of gear (or skin, in a real emergency).

Robert F. Thompson,
Traverse City, MI

A SHARP KNIFE IS A GOOD ONE

On a lengthy trip, carry a small whetstone for keeping your knives sharp. *Randolph E. Kerr, Albany, NY*

LASH WITH SHOCK CORDS

Elastic shock cords are nifty for securing a sleeping bag to a pack, if you're careful not to snag pack or bag with the wire hook ends on the cords. (You can file them smooth or cover with tape if you want to be really safe.)

Diana Weir, Salt Lake City, UT

KEEP YOUR DOWN DRY

A wet down sleeping bag is bad news, since it loses most of its insulative value. When camping in wet-weather country (such as the Pacific Northwest), take special precautions to avoid getting your down bag wet. Use inner and outer stuff sacks made of coated nylon with spring toggle closures. Seal all stuff sack seams with K-Kote or a similar sealant. Put the bag into the inner sack, then into the larger outer sack, with the closures at opposite ends to maximize protection. In addition to this careful bagging, air out your down bag as often as possible to rid it of moisture from your body and condensation inside the tent.

Tony Wright, Lake Oswego, OR

SECURE STORAGE

Sew D-rings inside the pockets of your pack or jacket for a handy, secure place to fasten car keys, etc.

Eleanor Adelman, Portland, OR

NO HOLES, PLEASE

When packing equipment, sleeping bag, etc. in a plastic trash bag, suck out all extra air before closing. This will prevent the bag from popping and exposing the equipment to the weather.   *Glenn Chokola, Colonia, NJ*

DRY IS BEAUTIFUL!

Put a large plastic bag (about the same dimensions as the inside of your pack sack) into the bottom of your pack. All clothes, cameras, etc. which must be kept dry can be put into it. Will withstand a complete dunking if the bag opening is twisted and closed with a strong rubber band.

Bill Straub, Pittsburgh, PA

FOR THE TRAVELER

Don't overlook those "travel containers and products" items in your department or drugstore. Frequently, there are great containers usable for backpacking (in the 50 cents to $1 range, some with squeeze tops), and you can often find neat little items such as tiny plastic clothespins, packets of towelettes, soaps, etc. The same manufacturers also put out a tiny sewing kit, collapsible razor, folding toothbrush, folding hairbrush, the small ½-ounce toothpaste tubes, and various other related items. Most are inexpensive and lightweight. I have especially used their little sewing kit and substituted the thread. I put in a piece or two of ripstop tape and I have a dandy repair kit that probably weighs about 1½ ounces.   *Carol Lloyd, Oakland, CA*

FREE SOAP

The small bars of soap found in motels are great for camping. (But not biodegradable, so please watch where you use them.)   *Tim Tackett, Russellville, AR*

ON TRIAL ON THE TRAIL

Keep your eyes open for trial-sized products in the drug,

discount, and variety stores. I have found deodorant, powder, shampoo, conditioner, toothpaste, soap, etc. in these neat little sizes. They are small, often reusable containers and usually weigh 1 or 1½ ounces . . . *great* for packing in your toilet kit.   *Carol Lloyd, Oakland, CA*

HEAVY DUTY REPAIRS

When repairing packing gear where sewing is involved, consider the following. Attachment (or reattachment) of a tie, strap, anchor, etc., should be done in a manner that prevents further damage or detachment. When sewing a strap to a pack or stuff sack, for example, back up the sewn area with a piece of heavy material or some of the strap. This will take the strain off the stitches somewhat and transfer it to the fabric and make rip-out less likely. For a strap-end attachment, sew an X in a "box," a pattern that will firmly anchor the strap.

For super strength, use a rivet set with a hammer. (Obtain from a leathercraft store.) Be sure it will comfortably accommodate the thickness of the attachment, including the backup. These rivets are great in the repair kit for emergencies. Set with two rocks, a flat one inside pack and a large oval one for the hammer. Another good addition to your emergency repair kit is a "Speedy Stitchery Sewing Awl" which sews heavy material with a lock stitch. It is available in some outdoor stores for about $2.   *Ted Lansing, Sepulveda, CA*

FIRST AID FOR ANKLES

The first aid kit should contain a rolled Ace bandage and an ankle bandage for people inclined to sprains. An ankle bandage is a tight-fitting sock with the toe area cut off. It is very convenient, since there is no bulky bandage around the ankle.   *Lorraine Kapakjian, Tenafly, NJ*

DAILY REMINDER

If you take any medication daily, pack the supply with your toothbrush or other gear you're likely to see and use each day.   *Happy Mulflur, Portland, OR*

CAN YOU SPARE A DIME?

Put 30 cents in your first aid kit for calls on a pay telephone en route to and from your trek. I put two dimes and two nickels in a coin collector's envelope and taped it to the lid of my first aid container. *Mike Westby, Portland, OR*

BACKBAND REPAIR

In 1975 the alloy of metal in the Kelty Mountaineer pack frame was changed to a cheaper combination of aluminum. This change led to premature failure of the lower padded backband where it touched the frame. The metal would undergo anodizing by sweat and wear away into small metal bits that abraded the backband at the frame contact points. When the backband ripped free of the frame in New Hampshire (only one month in my walk of the entire Appalachian Trail), I sewed two pieces of 2-inch-nylon "seat belt" webbing to the points to take the wear. This lasted well, all the way to Georgia. *Chris Kounkel, Spokane, WA*

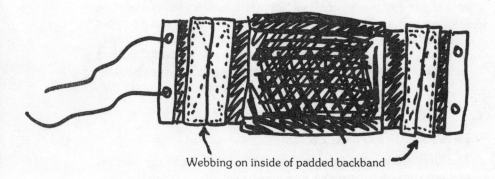

Webbing on inside of padded backband

WHEN THERE'S NO MORE ROOM

An adult's toothbrush weighs almost nothing, but its long handle can be unnecessary bulk to a trekker whose pack is fully loaded. Some of the alternatives available are: a child's toothbrush, a folding travel brush (you can even dispense with half the handle if you're really paring down), and a mini-version of an adult brush put out by PRO called "Double-Duty."

REFLECTIONS

A tiny hand mirror from a variety or drugstore costs 50 cents or less and can help you locate the bug or cinder in your eye, or even make a few repairs to your face or hair after days on the trail. (You may have the mirror half of a used-up pressed powder compact around.)   *Joan Ziegler, Portland, OR*

SOLVING THE WET OR DRY MYSTERY

You've been carrying wash-and-dry towelettes in your pack for a year and wonder if they've dried out or are still moist? Pop them into the freezer overnight. If they are crisp in the morning, they're still moist. If they're limp, they're not!
          J.G. Jarvis, Webster, NY

KEEPING YOUR CAMERA READY

Problem: How do you keep a 35mm camera handy, yet out of the way? *Solution:* I attach the shoulder strap of my camera to the top of my pack frame with a shower curtain ring. This makes it easy to totally detach the camera from the pack. The camera itself is held against my sleeping bag by an elastic cord which has been stretched out and attached at both ends. It's easy to slip this cord off the camera when I want to take a picture, and slip it over again afterwards, all with the pack still on my back.
          Steve Nadel, Middletown, CT

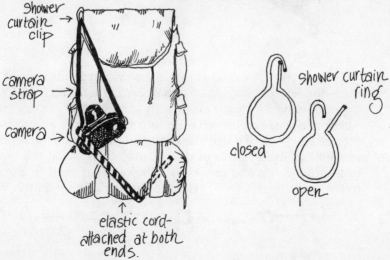

shower curtain clip

camera strap

camera

elastic cord- attached at both ends.

shower curtain ring

closed

open

I am a photographer and thus enjoy taking along a good camera. I also want the camera readily accessible in front of me and not buried in the pack. However, after about a day the constant weight on my neck gets to be a pain. To alleviate that, I have installed three small S-hooks on the pack to take the weight. One in the middle of the top bar holds the camera and one on each shoulder strap keeps the strap off the sides of my neck. I can bend over and do all normal motions (even falling down!) without losing the camera. The original camera strap was replaced with a nylon cord with hooks in each end to better fit into the S-hooks. If I intend to do any hiking without the pack, I take along a conventional camera strap.

To prevent the camera from bouncing around in front of me — and without buying an expensive camera hitch — I fixed up an adjustable 1-inch strap with snap hooks on each end. These are snapped onto the camera strap hooks and passed around my back. To use the camera I just unhook one hook and let the strap fall, take the picture, then swing the strap back around me and rehook it. Works great, and is cheap, too! *Robert Peterson, Binghamton, NY*

strap buckle   strap hook

A short, lightweight elastic shock cord can be looped around your camera or binoculars (worn on a strap around your neck) and hooked to your belt to keep the gear from flopping loosely.   *Paul Keller, Portland, OR*

WHEN YOU MUST CARRY A BIG WATER SUPPLY

In 1975 I walked the entire length of the Appalachian Trail from Maine to Georgia. On some parts of the trail, particularly in Pennsylvania and Tennessee, there was an acute shortage of water near the trail. Most of the time there, it was a long detour of two or three miles off the ridge to get to the water.

I found a very serviceable water carrier in a surplus store near my home in Illinois. It holds 5 quarts of water and has a pocket to place water purification tablets in (upper right corner). There are four sets of tie cords and webbing loops to tie to a pack frame on the nylon cover, and there is a polyethylene liner inside that holds the water. The official U.S. Army name is "Flotation Bladder, collapsible canteen, 5 quart." This item will also double as a float to help a person across a stream too deep to wade. The polyethylene liner can be removed from the nylon cover by unsnapping the three snaps at the right-hand side and pulling the liner out through the hole. Cost was $2.

Chris Kounkel, Spokane, WA

SENSIBLE STORAGE

Carry nightclothes and down jacket in your sleeping bag stuff sack.   *Dorothy Blattner, Portland, OR*

KEEPING YOUR FLASHLIGHT FLASHY

How can you keep your flashlight from turning on accidentally in your pack and wearing the batteries down? Either turn one battery around inside or pack the flashlight in your cooking pots; nestled in with the stove, all stay secure.

Ed and Claire Weiser, Villa Park, IL

PACKING YOUR BED

My summer sleeping gear—a 4¼-pound (total weight) fiberfill bag and a blue closed-cell foam pad—will fit in a 9-inch by 20-inch stuff sack if the pad is cut down to 18 inches by 36 inches. This makes a light (4¾-pounds) cheap sleeping system for summer. I can't stand to have things hanging all over my pack, so I want my foam pad in the stuff sack.   *Dusty Linder, Union, WA*

I never understood why most people pack their foam pads separate from their sleeping bags. I roll my pad around my sleeping bag and insert the somewhat larger than usual roll into a homemade vinyl-coated stuff sack. The package then fits neatly into the bottom space of my Kelty pack. The advantages are:
- all sleeping gear is together in one place
- the pad is protected from the rain
- the pad gives added protection to the sleeping bag
- the space formerly occupied by the pad alone can be used for something else
                                   Dieter Goetze, Santa Barbara, CA

PACK STRAP POCKET

On the shoulder strap of your pack, sew a small pocket to hold items frequently used while you're walking, such as sunglasses, map, compass, candy, etc.

Mike Westby, Portland, OR

TIES, LACES AND CORDS

Many times, a tie or lace will begin to fray at the end, although the rest of the cord is still good. If the application is such that melting the end will not be acceptable to stop this fraying (boot laces, etc.) or the cord is not nylon, try this. Completely dampen the frayed part (or cut back to solid cord and dampen the cut end) with white household glue (such as Elmer's Glue-All). Then wrap the end with a bit of tape, winding very tightly to make the tip as small as possible. When the glue is dry, the end will be tight and hard. You can remove the tape or not, as you wish.

Ted Lansing, Sepulveda, CA

TOTING YOUR FISHING GEAR

Lash your fishing rod or case to the side of your pack by securing it top and bottom with ½-inch-wide "rubber bands" cut from bike inner tubes. They are strong, and there is always enough tension present to hold the gear in place.　　　　　　　　　　*Hugh Brock, Portland, OR*

PRESERVE MAPS WITH MYLAR

Apply thin adhesive transparent mylar film to your maps for long-lasting protection. Applied to both sides, your map is practically indestructible. This method can also be used to protect driver's or fishing licenses and important directions. Buy Kwik Kover II (about $2 for a clear sheet 18 inches by 10 feet) at a discount or variety store, or similar products at an art supply department. The directions are helpful, but in the case of maps, the following tips are useful:

1. Straighten out map folds and lightly roll so that map is facing outside.

2. Cut out mylar and lay sticky side up on a flat smooth table or floor. Anchor mylar to flat surface so that it won't slip or wrinkle (double-sided sticky tape works best).

3. Carefully apply and align edge of map with edge of mylar and unroll map, smoothing out as you unroll. It is almost impossible to perfectly align the margins of map and mylar, so you may want to trim edges with a razor blade and straight-edge.

The mylar surface can't be imprinted with pencil, but a

fine-tipped washable felt pen works quite well for compass work and route plotting.   *Tony Wright, Lake Oswego, OR*

DESTINATION PRESERVATION

Maps and trail logs are important tools for the wilderness adventurer, but unless they're treated right, they can end up being useless. Whole lakes have been known to disappear on the worn-out folds of a much-used map!

One technique is to mount maps for trail use. Cut the map apart in sections along the grid lines and glue in place (with ½-inch margin between pieces) on cloth or flexible plastic. Your map can then be folded without wearing out along the folds. When in use, fold the map with the section you're traveling facing up, put the whole thing in a clear plastic bag to keep it dry and clean, and read through the plastic.

CUSTOMIZING A TRAIL GUIDEBOOK

In my trail guidebooks I underline in red all springs and in blue all shelters and/or campsites. This makes them ten times easier to spot. Believe me, it's a very worthwhile thing to do.   *David Carter, Ypsilanti, MI*

STREAMLINE MAPS

No sense carrying more weight than necessary, even when dealing with maps. Cut all extraneous paper from the U.S. Geological Survey quadrangle maps, taking care not to cut off any pertinent information. Also, make notes of convenient parking areas, items of interest along the way, etc. by using the backside of the quad. Use only an *indelible* felt-tipped marker to write in your comments, since this ink won't run when wet.   *Thomas M. Minchin, Brooklyn, NY*

FOUR-CENT MAP STORAGE

A one-gallon ziplock bag can be used for a map cover, and will also hold your trail log, extra paper, film, etc. all together in one handy dry place.
     Robert W. Love, Whitmore Lake, MI

MADE-TO-ORDER MAP CASE

Put rolled-up maps in the hollow tubing of your pack frame, then replace the rubber tip for easy storage.

Jon Carey, Dexter, MI

TEAMWORK!

Carry your map, compass, pencil and pad in an outside pocket that your hiking partner can easily reach.

Lorraine Kapakjian, Tenafly, NJ

GET THE HABIT!

When the toilet paper at home gets close to the end of the roll, take the cardboard tube out, flatten what's left and add it to your hiking supply in a plastic bag in your pack. You'll never run short on the trail because of forgetting to check your supply when getting ready for a trek.

Please also see these related ideas:

2.

Food Planning and Packaging

Folks contributed some very helpful ideas in this department, including ingenious ways to package foods that will save room in your pack, make preparation in camp easier, and reduce the amount of garbage that must be packed out. There are several fine recipes here to spark your appetites! If you are faced with the challenge of planning food for a long trip which requires food caches or pick-ups, others who have done long-distance trekking share their learnings.

The ideas in this section are those you'd employ before leaving home; in-camp techniques are dealt with in Chapter 10, Fixing and Feasting. For more ideas and details on the cooking/eating phase of wilderness travel, you might enjoy and find helpful my book The Well-Fed Backpacker.

HOME BAG-SEALING MACHINE A BOON

I have a few backpacking ideas that no one else taught me and which I have never or only once seen other hikers use. I have used them all with great success on my hike of the Appalachian Trail which has spanned three summer vacations and 1600 miles from Georgia to New Hampshire. I will complete the trail next summer, still using my techniques that have made the adventure run smoothly so far.

My all-time best idea is in food packaging and repackaging. All the ideas were born after I purchased a plastic bag sealer called "Meals in Minutes" from Sears for $15. I have used it many different ways for getting food drops ready to be mailed to me while I am hiking the AT. The primary use is to repackage freeze-dried food. I buy Rich-Moor food to serve four and then divide it three ways, using a triple beam balance, and seal each serving in one bag, trying to get as much air out as possible. As you know, Rich-Moor foods are wrapped in lots of garbage . . . one large bag to hold the noodles and the smaller gravy bag and meat bag. What I do is seal my Meals in Minutes bag vertically, making one pouch the right size to hold the gravy mix and the other pouch to hold noodles and meat. Since meatballs should be

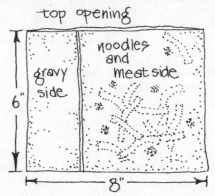

cooked longer than the gravy and noodles, I wrap them in Saranwrap to keep them separate. For chicken a la king I made one pouch for meat, one for gravy, and one for mashed potatoes. Experience will tell you how big to make the pouches. A funnel is used to put gravy or sauce mixes in the smaller pouches. When *all* the food is in the pouches, just seal across the top. I can tell by sight what is in the bag, and Rich-Moor's instructions for cooking are almost exactly the same for all their dinners, so I have that memorized, too. You can, however, write on the bags with a felt-tipped pen to label them, if necessary.

Another handy-dandy use is in the drink mix department . . . powdered milk, lemonade, iced tea, etc. What I do is figure out by taste how much powder to add to an amount of water that will just about fill my drinking cup. I find that a little less than ¾ of a cup of water plus the powder will make nearly a cup of drink. I then divide the plastic Meals in Minutes bag four or five times vertically. Then put the powder in, using a funnel, and seal across the top. With a 6-inch by 8-inch bag, you can only package three cups of powdered milk. With this technique you get a perfect mix every time with no guesswork. I also package one-quart drink mixes, two to a bag.

Last summer I hit on another idea for my little bags. I was having a hard time finding a cheap way to mail my peanut butter and honey. If I could just find a way besides a jar, I could save some postage (and the risk of breakage). Plastic containers cost money. Well, my little five-cent bags saved me again! I put enough peanut butter or honey in each bag to fill one Gerry tube. When I opened the food box, I would cut a small corner off the bag and squeeze the contents right into the Gerry tube. No messy knives or spoons! It worked great! If my Gerry tube wasn't quite empty yet, I'd put the bag of peanut butter or honey into my pack and carry it that way until the tube was empty and I could fill it up again. I strongly advise double-bagging these items, however. One of my boxes was soaked with honey, but it was a bad seal. After that my mom put the bags in a ziplock bag and there was no problem. *David Carter, Ypsilanti, MI*

Another hiker who has discovered what a help the home bag-sealer can be is Paul Downey of Nashville, TN.

Since powders for puddings, cream sauces, hot chocolate mix, milk, etc. begin to look very much alike after a few days in one's pack, a simple way of identifying can be done by writing the label, recipe or instructions on a small piece of paper and sealing it in the lower portion of the bag before it is filled with the powdered ingredients. One example is instant pistachio pudding with sliced almonds for a topping. The dry milk and a tablespoon of non-dairy creamer for added richness have been sealed in the main part of the bag with the pudding mix, and the nuts for topping in the other.

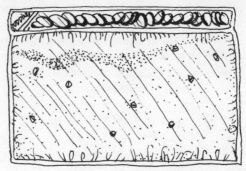

Just snip the top, pour the powder in a shaker bottle, add a pint of water, shake vigorously (violently) and after a few minutes serve with the sliced nuts on top. Easy and delicious!

Irene Luckham, of St. Petersburg, FL, relies on a bag-sealer also.

I find my electric bag sealer (mine is made by Oster, but I believe Dazey's Seal-a-Meal has been most publicized) is the best thing in my home when preparing for an overnight canoe or camping trip. Prepared food (stew, chili, etc.) is sealed in boilable bags and frozen. Come mealtime, just boil water and drop in the unopened bag. Your menu can be as endless as your imagination. We enjoyed pot roast, potatoes and carrots on an overnight canoe trip. The water used to boil the bags in can later be used for clean-up.

Dusty Linder of Union, WA, has her own system for using the bags.

Having some one-pot meals mixed up and ready to grab can be useful when preparing for a trip, but I've found they just don't keep very well in ordinary plastic bags, which seem to pick up moisture even sitting in a cupboard. The boilable-type bags sold for use with heat sealers are less permeable to air and thus keep the contents fresh longer. Write the directions on the bag with a sharp-pointed indelible felt pen. I keep my emergency food rations in one because it is less tempting to raid it when I have to tear it open and then redo it when I get home. I cut the bags into smaller sizes (you can buy a continuous roll at Sears and cut to suit) and seal the cut edges, making little packages. A 2-inch-square bag will hold a spoonful of coffee with milk and sugar, and is all ready to use (these should be labeled, to avoid surprises). I mix up a lot of these small packets at home at one time, then have a wide variety to choose from. In bigger groups, bulk packages make sense, but for one or two people on short trips you either drink one beverage exclusively or end up with a lot of half-used grimy bits to put away when you get home. I put up coffee substitute, Russian tea, mocha mix, cocoa, jello and Kool-Aid in these packets (the Kool-Aid is for snow cones).

BUY BABY BOTTLES BY THE ROLL

Playtex Nurser Bags are just the right size for repackaging almost everything. They are cheap (about $2 for a roll of 125) and tougher than freeze-dried pork chops! I use them to repackage powdered fruit drinks, soups, nuts, gorp, dried fruit, candy, margarine, sugar, dry milk, oatmeal, etc. They can be easily sealed with pipe cleaners cut into thirds with a pair of kitchen scissors or with the twist ties that come with various other kinds of plastic bags . . . rubber bands don't seem to work very well. Freezer tape can effect a pretty good closure. These little bags are *super!*

John Arrington, Poway, CA

STAPLES IN SERVING-SIZE PACKETS

Instead of carrying salt and pepper and sugar on a back-packing trip, whenever I go to one of the fast food places I pick up a few of the little paper packets that contain these staples. I can stuff the packets anywhere and everywhere on my person and in my backpack. They really come in handy when I need just a little sugar for my coffee or salt and pepper for dinner or a sandwich.

Marlene Schackmuth, Kenosha, WI

PASS THE SALT AND PEPPER, PLEASE

To save weight, space, and simplify kitchen procedures on the trail: mix salt and pepper together at home to your taste.

John H. Gamble, Morgantown, WV

The perfect camping and backpacking salt shaker is an "Adolf's Meat Tenderizer" plastic container. It holds a good quantity (which the clever but too-small commercial shakers don't) and has a sturdy cap to keep out moisture, besides being unbreakable. Just pry off the perforated top and fill with salt or salt and pepper mixed.

George Bernard David, Wallingford, CN

JUST MY SIZE!

Watch your grocery store for the many food items that can be found from time to time in the trial-size packages . . . especially cereals, seasonings, cooking oil, and related items. *Carol Lloyd, Oakland, CA*

IF YOU SHUN POWDERED EGGS

Fresh eggs can be carried safely for a day or two in mild weather, and you needn't carry them in the bulky plastic cartons. Break the eggs into a ziplock bag, seal it, after pushing out as much air as possible, and tuck the packet in with your eating/cooking gear for protection from pokes and squeezes. *Happy Mulflur, Portland, OR*

NON-STICK COOKING

Before you leave for a hike, spray the pan you plan to cook dinner in with one of the vegetable oil sprays (such as Pam or Cooking Ease). Food will not stick and the pan is much easier to clean. (*Don't* coat the pan you plan to heat water in!) *Bill Straub, Pittsburgh, PA*

FILL 'ER UP!

At home I keep my extra fuel bottle (used only for longer trips, and most of mine are short) filled with a funnel from the big gas can. Then when I get home I can refill the stove from the little bottle . . . a lot easier than trying to pour from the big can. *Dusty Linder, Union, WA*

REDUCE FOIL BULK

Remove the bulky foil packaging from freeze-dried foods when packing for your treks. Place contents in a resealable plastic bag or use your heat sealing machine. If the freeze-dried food is to be prepared by simply pouring boiling water on it, you may want to leave it in the inner tough plastic bag it comes in, with the cardboard stiffener on the base. Then just slip food and bag (with instructions if needed) into an airtight plastic bag.

REMEMBER THE CAN OPENER?

Put a GI can opener on your set of car keys. You'll always have your car keys with you, even though you don't have, or forgot, a can opener.   *Mike Westby, Portland, OR*

AU NATUREL

For vegetarians a small hand mill works great to crack brown rice, millet, barley, wheat, etc. for soups that take 10 minutes to cook instead of 30. Prepackaged at home with spices, they make a more nutritious meal than the white-flour content of most freeze-dried meals. Natural food stores carry whole wheat noodles and other pastas, too.
Margarite Hoefler, Kansas City, MO

Muesli is a good breakfast which saves fuel and can be made to suit one's own taste. Mix all the ingredients when preparing food for the trip. To use it, set the amount for breakfast to soak the night before. The dried foods become easily chewed and digested by soaking up water; cooking is not needed. A one-pint cottage cheese container with a tight-fitting lid works well as a bowl for one person. The following is a general recipe for one serving (soak in ¾-cup water). Vary the kinds of grains, fruits and nuts according to what's available and what you want.

1 tablespoon rolled grain
¼ to ½ cup dried fruit

1 tablespoon seeds or nuts
1 to 2 tablespoons milk powder

Yes, it really is just a tablespoon of grain per serving. This is a Scandinavian dish which is primarily fruit and milk. In the home, fresh fruit and milk would be used.

Similar mixes can be soaked for dinner (put them in a watertight container in the morning). According to your own taste, combine rolled grains, seeds or nuts, dried vegetables, and seasonings. For example:

Soak in ¾ cup water, for 1 serving:

¼ cup rye flakes
1 tablespoon sunflower seeds
½ cup dried cabbage
1 teaspoon vegetable bouillon
caraway seeds and basil

Suzanne Smith, Portland, OR

Grains and beans can be sprouted while hiking. Put them in a drawstring bag made of nylon net or other sheer nylon material. Soak overnight, drain, and rinse several times a day. The bag can be hung from the pack in wet or humid weather or put in a plastic bag to protect the sprouts from drying out. If sprouting is going slowly due to cold weather, the sprouts can be eaten at an earlier stage than you would normally.

Suzanne Smith, Portland, OR

FORAGED GOODIES GUIDE

The study and use of wild edible plants adds a new dimension to my enjoyment of the outdoors, but when I have a fully loaded pack, I often don't want to carry a guidebook with me. After I've learned to recognize an edible plant, the thing I often have trouble remembering is how to *use* it. Is it good raw in salads? Do I make tea out of it? Is it edible in only a certain stage of maturity? So I made a sort of local abstract for the most common edible plants found in the areas I usually roam, based on Donald Kirk's *Wild Edible Plants of the Western United States*. Here are samples of some of my two-page lightweight guide, showing the main headings and a few plants under each:

Berries (eat raw, stewed, in pies and cobblers)
  Oregon grape
  manzanita
  serviceberry
  salal

Teas (if using leaves, either fresh or dried, not in between)
  hemlock (needles)
  Scotch broom (roasted seeds)
  clover (dried flowers)
  yarrow (dried entire plant)
  strawberry (leaves)

Juice
  prince's pine (boil roots and leaves)
  squawbush (soak berries, lemony taste)

Roots/bulbs (roast or boil)
  cattail
  deer fern
  bear grass
  wild onion
  thistle

Flowers and buds
  raw: prickly pear cactus
        Indian paintbrush
        clover
  boiled: chickweed
          wild rose
          sweet coltsfoot
          Oregon grape

Nuts
  acorns (some need tannin leached out): grind for flour
  chinquapin
  hazelnut

Soup (either solely of wild goodies, or add to prepared soup)
  fern fiddleheads
  fireweed (pith of stems)
  valerian (roots)

wild onion
pepper grass (seeds)

Asparagus alternatives
fern fiddleheads
peeled cattail shoots
young milkweed shoots

Cooked greens (tender leaves, young shoots best)
watercress
nettles
plantain

Raw greens (salads)
wood sorrel
cow parsnip (peeled young stems)
miner's lettuce

BALANCING THE BULK

When we take to the woods we often don't get the bulk and
roughage we normally do from salads and fresh vegetables.
To solve this problem and also get a large helping of energy
plus a filling, stick-with-you breakfast, I prepackage a large
helping of a natural high-bulk cereal such as Nature Valley
Granola or Kellogg's Country Morning. I add raisins, nuts
and powdered milk and put it all in a large plastic baggie.

When I'm ready to eat breakfast in camp, I add water and a squirt of honey. I knead the baggie until all the ingredients are mixed, then eat directly from the bag. When I build my campfire that night, I burn the bag. It's all fast and neat and I don't have to mess around with lighting my stove. Of course, if you are cost-conscious or prefer a special recipe, you could start with your own homemade granola.

Ron Youngs, Mt. Carmel, IL

And if you do want a hot breakfast and have water going for coffee, simply empty the baggie's contents into your bowl, pour hot water over, and mix well.

BACKCOUNTRY SALADS

We pack with our horses for days or weeks. One of the things that works beautifully for us is to grate up carrots and cabbage and put them in plastic containers. These salad basics last and stay exceedingly fresh for almost two weeks. When it is hot, we put the containers in a spring at night; backpackers could also store them in cool water like a lake. We carry the other ingredients for salad—raisins, small marshmallows—in individual plastic bags premeasured for each meal. A small can of crushed pineapple, an apple, and some mayonnaise go along so we can make coleslaw or waldorf salad. In hot weather the perishable ingredients should be carried in the center of a pack for best insulation.

Marian B. Crumb, Hayden Lake, ID

ELEGANT APPETIZERS

An elegant, simple, high-protein snack (or appetizer before your one-pot dinner): pack cream cheese (try the kind with pimientos or chives) in a plastic tube and thin slices of Armour's beef (comes in a jar) in a sandwich baggie. Spread cream cheese on each meat slice and roll it up.

Marilyn Anderson, Portland, OR

A WAY TO CARRY FRESH MEAT

Situation: You want to take hamburger on a trip, but the weather is hot and the meat won't keep well; you also don't want heavy foods. *Solution:* Precook the hamburger and drain off the fat to reduce the weight of the meat. Wrap the cooked hamburger in plastic and aluminum foil and put it in the freezer. Just before you load your pack for a trip, wrap the frozen meat package in newspaper and put it in the bottom of your pack to insulate it. This frozen hamburger will keep much longer than fresh meat and is easier to cook with in camp.   *Herbert W. Kruger, Portland, OR*

NO-SMASH, TASTY BREAD

Bagels make good hiking bread! They are heartier and tastier than many crackers, travel extremely well even crammed inside a pack. They can be toasted or eaten with many spreads such as cheese, peanut butter, jam, cream cheese.   *Elizabeth Handler, Portland, OR*

DESSERT EXTRAS

To brighten up our meals when backpacking, we carry dry skim milk in small baggies, a variety of instant puddings, some extras to top the puddings, and a one-quart plastic shaker. Some of the toppings we use are: bright-colored sprinkles (used for cake decorating), cinnamon red hots, M & M candies, colored coconut, chopped nuts, raisins, chopped dried fruits.   *L. Max Madry, Orlando, FL*

HIGH COUNTRY DAIQUIRIS

I can't take credit for the original recipe, but here's the way I do High Country Daiquiris. The adaptations are mine and believe me, they can add a lot to a trip.

Before you leave town, ration out 155 proof rum. That's right, 155 proof. It's so potent you don't have to carry so much and a little goes a long way at 6,000 feet or so elevation. I figure ¾ ounce per person per day. Put it in a plastic flask. Also take along some dry daiquiri mix, the kind you buy in the supermarket. I use a coffee pot for my mixer. Make a paste of the dry mix and some water in the pot, add the rationed rum, fill the pot with snow, dance a wild Indian dance around the campfire as you mix the daiquiris. I find the war chant is best, but the rain chant will do, even though it's risky.

By the time the dancer is exhausted, the daiquiris are mixed, so into the sierra cups it goes. Ah, nice. Sit on a log and toast the gods that brought you here.

One small warning. *Really* ration the rum. I poured a friend one of these daiquiris a couple of years ago. She sipped it, remarked, "Oh, it's so lovely up here," got up and walked right into Moccasin Lake in the Wallowas.

Dan Sellard, Eugene, OR

A FROZEN DELICACY IN THE HIGH COUNTRY

On a recent two-month hike on the Pacific Crest Trail, we always carried Tang orange-flavored drink powder with us. We would frequently scoop up a bowl of snow crystals (not the powdery stuff), add two tablespoons of Tang and stir it up. It made a delicious form of "Italian ices" especially welcome after climbing a long distance up to a mountain pass from a hot valley.   *Simeon Ross, Smithtown, NY*

QUANTITY-PACKAGING OF HOME-CONCOCTED DINNERS

Like many backpackers, I don't enjoy freeze-dried foods very much, and I find them too expensive, besides. For dinners, I get the following ingredients at a supermarket and combine them into six or eight individual servings.

1 pound macaroni	.39
14 ounces quick rice	.79
3 ounces dried soup greens or other vegetables	.99
1 ounce dried parsley flakes	.43
2 boxes Lipton's Make-A-Better Burger or other soy protein product such as Proteinettes	1.09
dry soup mix enough to make two quarts (bouillon, Cup-A-Soup, etc.)	1.00
salt, pepper, spices to taste	.10
	4.79

These ingredients will make about 24 cups of cooked food. Decide how many meals you want (usually six 4-cup meals for very heavy eaters or eight 3-cup meals for average on-the-trail appetites) and open that many ziplock bags. Into each bag, put equal amounts of all the ingredients (except the rice and macaroni), one tablespoon of salt, and spices to taste. The rice and macaroni each get divided among half the bags (3 or 4 rice meals, 3 or 4 macaroni).

To cook, add 2 cups water (2½ for the larger meals) to the ingredients in a pot, bring to a boil and simmer gently for about 10 minutes, stirring occasionally.

For interest I vary the soups (thick soups such as cream of mushroom work best) and spices, often add some fresh vegetables (carrots keep up to 10 days in moderate weather, other vegetables 4 or 5 days), or maybe even some hard salami that doesn't need refrigeration.

The cost for each basic meal is 60 cents if you make eight meals, 80 cents if you make six. The soy protein provides protein, the vegetables give you vitamins and minerals, and the rice or macaroni is largely carbohydrates . . . a well-balanced combination, providing abundant calories.

Steve Nadel, Middletown, CN

HIKER'S SAUSAGE

5   pounds of the least expensive ground beef
5   teaspoons Tender Quik Curing Salt (Morton's)
2½ teaspoons garlic salt
1   teaspoon Hickory Smoked Salt (French's)
2½ teaspoons coarse ground pepper
2½ teaspoons mustard seed
other seasonings as you like, such as red pepper

Mix all spices together. Crumble the hamburger, slowly mix in the spices. Cover, refrigerate for 24 hours.

Second day: Mix again; refrigerate another 24 hours.

Third day: Form into five rolls 8 inches long and 2 inches in diameter. Put on rack two inches apart and put in oven. Bake eight hours at 150 degrees, turning rolls every two hours.

This sausage costs about 50 cents a roll, is delicious and keeps quite a while without refrigeration. It can also be stored in the refrigerator or freezer with no loss of flavor.

Mary Morris, Portland, OR

TRAVEL WITH A BAKERY

Many different baked goods can be turned out on the trail without a reflector oven, if you use the ring mold oven technique. Either purchase the commercial oven made by Optimus or make your own (see page 170). Try Bisquik coffee cakes (recipes on the box), stir and frost cake mixes, and a delicious fruit-studded cake made by pouring water on freeze-dried fruits, then adding Bisquik until you have a batter.   *Robert W. Love, Whitmore Lake, MI*

RUM-RAISIN PUDDING . . . MMMMMM!

Here is a recipe for pudding my children particularly enjoy.

The dry ingredients called for can be packaged by the home bag-sealing method (described on pages 43-47.)

Package together at home:
1   small package instant vanilla or French vanilla pudding
⅔ cup instant dry milk
1   tablespoon non-dairy creamer
On the trail:
1   handful raisins
6   to 8 drops rum flavoring
¼ cup water

Preparation: During the first rest break after lunch, put the raisins, rum flavoring, and water in a short wide-mouthed container (such as is used for cheese or margarine). Screw the top on tightly, toss it in your pack and let it jostle there while you walk the rest of the afternoon. (All that gentle shaking will make the raisins nice and plump.) When dinnertime rolls around, pour the dry ingredients in a wide-mouthed pint shaker bottle, add one cup water and shake vigorously for a few seconds. Add the raisins/rum flavoring/water and shake again. Add enough more water to make one pint, shake again and put in a cold spring or snow bank (if you're that lucky) until supper is done. A little extra work, but the results are definitely worth it.

Paul L. Downey, Nashville, TN

MARIAN'S ENERGY COOKIES

Here's a hearty trail cooky that loves to travel, keeps well, and is chock full of nutrition. This recipe makes 11 to 12 dozen large cookies, so you can freeze some to have ready for later trips. We have almost completely replaced candy bars and gorp with these cookies. Nearly everyone who tastes one asks for the recipe!

8   cups quick rolled oats
2½ cups sugar
1   tablespoon ground ginger
2   cups melted vegetable shortening
2   cups light molasses

4   beaten eggs
¼   cup hot water
8½   cups sifted flour
1   tablespoon salt
2   tablespoons baking soda
3   cups raisins
2   cups chopped walnuts

In a *large* bowl or dishpan, mix oatmeal, sugar and ginger. Stir in melted shortening, molasses, beaten eggs and hot water. Sift in dry ingredients, reserving ½ cup flour. Add raisins and nuts. Mix dough with hands until well mixed. Add the ½ cup of flour if needed to make dough workable (it will work more easily if mixed while still warm . . . the warmer the better). Roll portions of the dough to ¼-inch thickness; cut with cookie or biscuit cutter. Place cookies on lightly greased baking sheet. Bake about 9 or 10 minutes at 350 degrees. Makes 11 to 12 dozen large cookies.

Marian B. Crumb, Hayden Lake, ID

NIBBLES FOR NOURISHMENT

For quick energy and food value on the trail, I nibble off and on all day on a good-tasting mountain mix. Doing this, I usually do not need any lunch, so only pack meals for breakfast and supper. My basic recipe is:

1 pound each: raisins
              salted peanuts
              semi-sweet chocolate chips

Mix together well. You can also add sunflower seeds, other dried fruits, or whatever else your taste buds enjoy.

Tom Hopkins, Arras, British Columbia, Canada

GRILLED FLANK STEAK

This delicious recipe has been used dozens of times in many situations, with raves all around! It can be served with quick-cooking Japanese noodles.

⅓   cup dry red wine
2   tablespoons cooking oil
1/8   teaspoon garlic powder

dash cayenne pepper
1/4   cup soy sauce
1/4   teaspoon monosodium glutamate
1/8 teaspoon ground ginger

Combine all ingredients at home. Let a large piece of flank steak marinate in the mixture for 15 minutes, then roll meat and pack in a clean one-quart milk carton. Pour in marinade, allowing 1/2 inch space at the top for expansion. Cut down top of carton if need be. Fold, seal with freezer tape, and freeze.

To take in backpack for your first or second night out, be sure to place the carton in a plastic bag which you seal for extra protection. In camp drain marinade off meat and cook quickly on grill over coals or in a pan on a camp stove. Don't overcook. Cut diagonally in thin strips to serve.

Ginger Peterson, Bend, OR

MEATLESS MEAT LOAF

This recipe makes about 10 slices, keeps a couple of days even in warm weather, may be eaten hot or cold. We've found this delicious for a nice filling dinner after hiking many hours. It makes a great variation from salami for lunch!

6   cups Kellogg's Special K cereal
5   beaten eggs
1/3 cup oil
1   pint ricotta cheese
1   4-serving package onion soup mix

Mix all ingredients together well, pour into greased loaf pan, bake 45 minutes to 1 hour at 350 degrees, till browned well. Refrigerate till you leave for your hike. Just slice and eat. Hearty and delicious!   *Jan Walker, Baltimore, MD*

BEEF IT UP

The Natural Foods Backpack Dinners made in Oregon have

exotic and delicious flavors because of the ingenious combinations of vegetables, grains and spices. If you're one who likes meat in his meals, you can simply add sausage, fresh meat, freeze-dried meat, bacon or meat bar (from the outdoor store), or even textured vegetable protein to make these excellent meals even heartier and extend each package to one more serving. The 20 minutes cooking time required for most of the Natural Foods Backpack Dinners will amply rehydrate TVP or freeze-dried meat. You may need to add a little more water.

BEEF STEW AND DUMPLINGS

At home: In a plastic baggie, put 2 cups Bisquik and ¼ cup powdered milk. In another baggie, put 1 package vegetable beef soup mix, ½ package beef stew seasoning, and dried onions and other vegetables as desired.

In camp: Bring 5 cups water to a boil, add the soup/ seasonings/vegetables. Add about ⅔-cup water to the Bisquik mix in its bag, mix till a stiff dough is formed, and drop by spoonfuls onto the boiling stew. Cook 10 minutes uncovered over low heat, then cover and cook 10 minutes more.

This is delicious and plenty for three people, the number usually in my group. Two really hearty eaters can finish it off, but they won't need any dessert then! (For additional protein, you can package ¼-cup of textured vegetable protein with the soup mix, or crumble part of a precooked, compressed meat bar into the bubbling stew.)

Helen R. Arnold, Lebanon, PA

CROOKED RIVER BREAKFAST (serves 2)

This trail treat is named after the place we first enjoyed it. It is a delicious and hearty breakfast for a day when you're not in a hurry to be off (it could also be a nice mainstay for a leisurely dinner). It requires two cook pots, one shallow; our Sigg Tourister kit is perfect, as we can put two pots on the stove simultaneously.

The meal consists of two parts: a giant herb-flavored biscuit and a rich sauce with ham. It allows many variations for your personal taste preferences.

Sauce
(larger pot)

Add ¼ cup dried tomatoes and 1 chicken bouillon cube to water (amount varies; see below). Simmer till tomatoes are rehydrated and bouillon is dissolved.

Then add sauce packet (see variations, below), dry milk (in amount needed to produce the amount of liquid milk specified on packet), and ham pieces (can be freeze-dried ham, leftover ham from home, bacon bits, or ham-flavored textured vegetable protein; if you use TVP, add it to water along with tomatoes, so it can soften).

Simmer till sauce is thick and ham is warmed through.

Sauce
Variations

For the basic flavoring of the sauce, use any of the supermarket sauce mixes that you like; we have enjoyed hollandaise, cheese, and sour cream. Follow directions on back of the packet to determine the amount of water and dry milk you'll need. The mixes usually produce one fluid cup of sauce, and that is enough for two people.

Biscuit
(shallow pan)

Mix together at home:
1 cup biscuit mix (like Bisquik)
2 tablespoons dry milk
1 teaspoon dehydrated onion flakes
a bit of your favorite herbs: basil, oregano, tarragon, whatever

In camp:
Add ¼ cup water to biscuit mix, mix well.

To Cook

Melt a generous blob of margarine in your shallow pan. Spread the biscuit mix in, patting the top smooth with your hand. When it's thoroughly brown and cooked on one side, turn over, adding more margarine if needed, and cook on flip side. It should be crusty brown and buttery on both sides. The finished product is the size of a very large pancake, but the thickness and texture of a biscuit.

If you have a cook kit that allows you to use two pots at once, start the sauce, then put the second pot on top and "bake" the biscuit while the sauce simmers. If you have to juggle pans, boil the water, throw in the tomatoes and bouillon cube, set aside while you do the biscuit, then finish the sauce. If the biscuit cools a bit, it doesn't matter; but cold sauce is yucky.

To serve   Break the biscuit into sierra-cup-size pieces and pour sauce over. Or if you're feeling friendly, sit close together and eat out of the pan.

Martha Stuckey, Portland, OR

The following ideas might also be used when you are planning and packaging trail food:

3

Make It Yourself

A small investment of time can result in big savings and custom equipment . . . just the way you want it, to do exactly the job you need. Using a piece of gear you've made yourself is pleasing not just because it functions well, but also because the creative, clever part of you has had a fun workout!

Here are many dandy ways not only to save money, but in many cases to improve on the equipment that is available . . . . Oneupmanship at its best!

HOMEMADE SANDWICH PAD

After purchasing an open-celled foam pad, I found I need a close-celled foam pad for warmth, so I cut the 3/8'' ensolite a little smaller than the open-celled pad and put it inside the cloth cover. One roll incorporates comfort and warmth, and two (or four, if they're available) sturdy arms can roll it into a very small roll. (A few commercially-made ''sandwich pads'' are on the market, but you can certainly save a few coins by putting together your own.)

Margarite Hoefler, Kansas City, MO

IMPROVING THE CLOSED-CELL PAD

Your closed-cell foam pad can do good things for you, or not, depending on the circumstances. If you have found yourself off the pad at night due to a sloped campsite or whatever, try this.

Get enough waterproof ripstop nylon to make a cover for the pad, as shown. Sew three or four ties to the cover and to your sleeping bag so they can be tied together. (You might prefer to use velcro.) Then pad and bag will not separate when in use. I added a pocket at one end which I stuff with my down parka for a perfect pillow which will not slip out from under my head at night. I also cut my pad so that one piece is perfect for a sit-upon. I use it for that purpose until I go to bed, when it again becomes part of my sleeping system. The sit-upon part can be enclosed in a plastic bag while in use for that purpose, but this isn't really necessary.

Ted Lansing, Sepulveda, CA

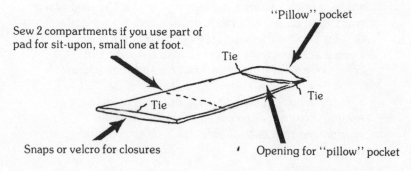

Sew 2 compartments if you use part of pad for sit-upon, small one at foot.

"Pillow" pocket

Tie

Tie

Tie

Snaps or velcro for closures

Opening for "pillow" pocket

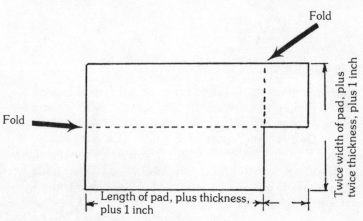

Fold

Fold

Length of pad, plus thickness, plus 1 inch

Twice width of pad, plus twice thickness, plus 1 inch

HANGING TOILET KIT FOR PENNIES

Want a neat way to keep your toilet kit organized and be able to hang it up? So did I. I got tired of always having to lay it down on something and not being able to hang it on a tree limb or whatever. Take two *sturdy* ziplock bags of the one-quart size (double the bags if you don't have the heavier commercial variety). Cut a 2-inch strip of pack cloth or coated taffeta and sew the strip to the *bottom* of one bag and to the outside of the back of the other bag near the top edge. Sew a *small* piece of fabric on the top of the top bag and put a grommet in it. Attach a string or shoelace, and you have a two-compartment hanging toilet kit. Fold it over and tie it together, and it is ready for packing. Since it is mostly plastic, it cleans easily and you can see exactly what's in it. To make it stronger, put a piece of ripstop tape (or duct tape or adhesive tape) over the pieces where you have stitched.

Carol Lloyd, Oakland, CA

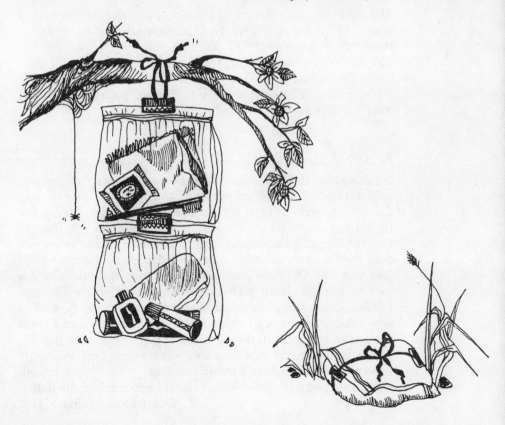

COMPASS CASE FROM SCRAPS

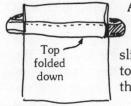

Top folded down

A simple case for your compass can be made in a few minutes from a scrap of waterproof nylon packcloth. It is used by sliding in the compass and folding down the top, then wrapping the velcro tape around the case to hold the compass secure.

Chris Kounkel, Spokane, WA

COVER YOUR OWN PAD

I covered my foam sleeping pad with urethane-coated nylon. It is now waterproof and has a smoother surface, so my sleeping bag doesn't cling to the pad when I turn over.

Helen R. Arnold, Lebanon, PA

The cost to make your own covered open-celled foam pad is about $7.50 for a shorty pad (compared to $12.95 for a ready-made one) and $13.65 for a full-length one (versus $17.50). And when you buy the coated nylon needed for your cover (45 inches wide, 1⅓ yards for a 48-inch pad cover and 3 yards for a 72-inch cover), you'll have enough fabric left over to make several small stuff sacks!

AN ORGANIZER FOR YOUR COOKING GEAR

A Svea stove doesn't really need to be in a sack (unless you prime it by lighting paper under it, thus getting it sooty, a la Colin Fletcher). But the little coated nylon stuff sack I made for mine is just great, because it keeps all the small parts together. I sewed a piece of elastic to the inside of the sack to hold the cleaner, pot handle, and eyedropper for priming. (If you use the Optimus mini-pump instead, it could also be tucked into the elastic.) There's room in the bag for a lighter (which solves the problem of what to do with burnt matches when you don't have a fire), a small circle of closed-cell foam for under-stove insulation, a piece of foil to use as a pot lid, and a small box of matches in a plastic bag. All this stuff used to get lost before I made the bag—now I know it's all there ready to use. (All I have to do is keep track of the bag!)

Dusty Linder, Union, WA

PORTABLE WOOD-BURNING STOVE

I have developed a small wood-burning backpacking stove which is portable and very easy to use. It can be built with simple hand tools from sheet steel. This stove represents a real breakthrough in cooking for backpackers. It weighs less than a conventional gas stove (including a can of fuel). It never runs out of fuel. You can cook on a much smaller amount of wood than with a conventional fire. My stepson carried one version of the stove with him when he hiked the Appalachian Trail this past summer, and he is a total convert to it!   *Frank Bequaert, Lexington, MA*

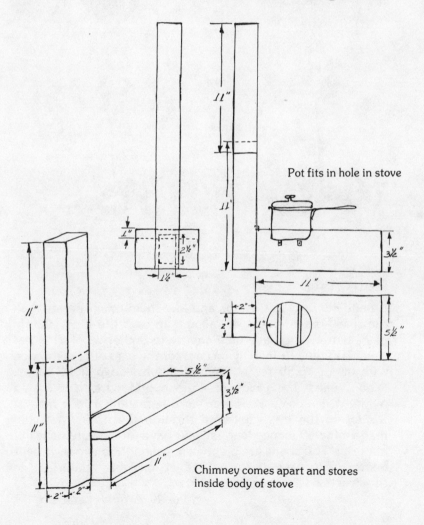

Pot fits in hole in stove

Chimney comes apart and stores inside body of stove

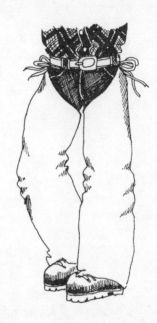

"Store-bought" rain chaps (below) have two ties, require a belt. Homemade variety (left) has only one tie, needs no belt, is cheaper too.

RAIN CHAPS

I made my own rain chaps and like them much better than the ready-made ones. Mine come up over the hips, stay in place better, and have only one tie to bother with. The cost was $4.13 plus ¼ inch nylon cord for the waist tie, compared with about $6.50 for a commercially-made pair of chaps. (You'll need 1½ yards of 45-inch wide urethane-coated nylon, which costs $2.75 per yard.) I made a 1-inch hem at the top to run the waist cord through. I am 5'6" tall and made mine 40 inches long, so you have an extra 5 inches of material. The chaps are plenty wide enough to slip over your boots. The seams do not ravel on this material, so construction is simple and quick.

Helen R. Arnold, Lebanon, PA

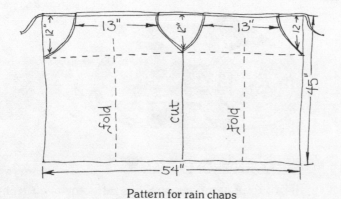

Pattern for rain chaps

UNSTUFFING SIMPLIFIED

Stuff bags supplied with parkas and sleeping bags are usually designed to make the most compact storage possible when in use. However, it is often nearly impossible to remove the contents when so solidly packed, especially when wearing gloves or mittens. To improve this situation, obtain an amount of 1-inch-wide flat webbing which will reach across the bottom of the stuff bag when full, plus approximately 2 inches more. While the bag is full, place the webbing across the bottom of the bag, and up each side about 1 inch. Mark the position of the ends of the strap on the bag with felt pen. Then, unpack the bag and sew the ends of the strap in the locations marked. Add a piece of strap inside to reinforce the stitching, and add a rivet for strength. This strap will provide a handhold for unpacking the bag when stuffed tight.   *Ted Lansing, Sepulveda, CA*

REFLECTOR OVEN FROM A CAN

For a small group of campers, make a reflector oven from a #10 can, snipped and bent in a few places. The "shelf" on which food is placed to bake can be made of heavy-duty foil.

STUFF SACK ORGANIZERS

Make stuff sacks for your gear in various sizes and colors from remnants of coated nylon purchased at fabric or outdoor stores. Use shoelaces and spring toggles for the drawstring closures, and label either permanently by writing on the sacks with indelible felt-tipped pen, or temporarily by affixing masking tape that lists contents of each bag. Friends could each buy one or two yards of one color, and swap some so everyone ends up with an assortment.

Joan Ziegler, Portland, OR

TWO-PART CLOTHING BAG

When sewing your own stuff sacks for clothing, include a full-length fabric divider down the middle. As clothes get dirty, they can be stored together in one half of the bag (not spread to various corners of your pack). Thus, your stuff sack remains full and comfortable when it doubles as a pillow.

Jim Andrews, Portland, OR

CUSTOM COLORS FOR YOUR GEAR

I have designed and made quite a lot of our clothing. I

choose soft, muted outdoorsy colors because I don't like to be gaudy. But sometimes you need bright colors for safety, so our 60/40 cloth parkas are dull-colored on the outside, but have blaze orange linings. They can be turned inside out and worn in an emergency, laid on snow as a marker, or waved.

Dusty Linder, Union, WA

MONSTER BOOT

MONSTER BOOTS

To wear while loafing around the snow camp.

1. *Insulated insole:* Trace around the foot which will want to live in this boot . . . assume two pairs of fat socks. Then, use this pattern to cut two layers out of a closed-cell foam sleeping pad (or use the soles of old ''thong'' sandals) and glue together (waterproof glue, of course).

2. *Rim:* Now cut a long strip of foam, about 1 inch wide, and glue and sew with an awl to the insole. Make the part around the heel about 2 inches high, so when you're sitting around the campfire and watching it slowly sink into the snow, your heels will stay warm as they rest in the snow.

3. *Sole:* Cut out a sole from a *rough* fabric (we used canvas), same outline as your assembled insole with rim, plus 5/8 inch seam allowance all sides.

4. *Uppers:* For each Monster Boot, cut 2 uppers out of waterproof nylon fabric; with *right* sides together, stitch center front seam. Sew a piece of elastic about 3 inches long across the top of the foot. Stitch the center back seam. *Then* carefully stitch the whole thing to the canvas sole.

5. *Finishing touches:* Turn right side out. Insert the insole and try on for fit. Hem the top edge (insert a drawstring if it seems too sloppy). Finally, sew the eye from a hook-and-eye-fastener on the top front of the Monster Boot. This is for securing your "Gators," next . . . .

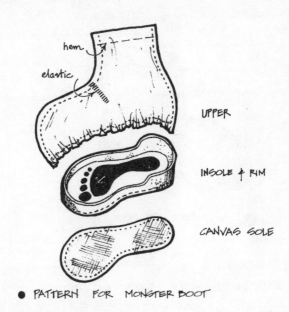

● PATTERN FOR MONSTER BOOT

"GATORS"

1. *Patterns:* Have your leg handy for measuring. Draw your pattern based on the sole-to-top-of-boot distance and top-of-boot-to-knee distance. Then measure around your leg and shoe at these three places, remembering to allow for bulky winter clothing. Also allow for hems and seams and a casing at the top.

2. *Assembly:* Sew center front seam. Hem the sides and bottom edges. Cut a piece of fabric about 1¼ inches wide for the elastic casing, press under the edges, and sew *inside* the Gator. Also, fold down the top to form a casing on the inside.

3. *Fasteners:* Sew velcro strips to the side opening. Try on the Gator, and measure length for the strap under the boot. Sew on strap; insert elastic and tack at the ends; insert a drawstring. Finally, sew on hook from a hook-and-eye fastener to the center front; this hooks into your boot lace to

hold the Gator down, *and* also hooks onto your Monster Boot, after you've taken off your ski boots and are lounging around the snow camp with warm toes.

Recommended fabric for Gators: waterproof nylon (snow won't stick and water won't soak in). Total construction time for Monster Boots and Gators: one evening.

Martha Andrews, Portland, OR

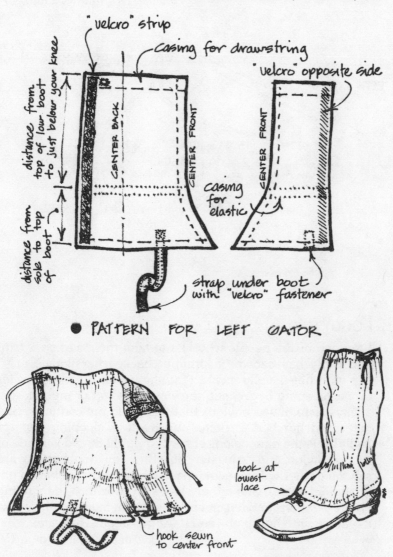

"velcro" strip

casing for drawstring

"velcro" opposite side

distance from top of low boot to just below your knee

CENTER BACK

CENTER FRONT

CENTER FRONT

casing for elastic

distance from sole to top of boot

strap under boot with "velcro" fastener

● PATTERN FOR LEFT GATOR

hook sewn to center front

hook at lowest lace

● ASSEMBLED GATOR

● GATOR

SUPER LIGHTWEIGHT FISHING RIG

To make this simple, very lightweight fishing rig, predrill a hole in the end of a tent pole or clip a large safety snap over the fork on the end of a branch. Fifteen yards of leader on its plastic packaging spool is fastened to the "pole" by means of a rubber band around a twig.

Howard Hoffman, Vallejo, CA

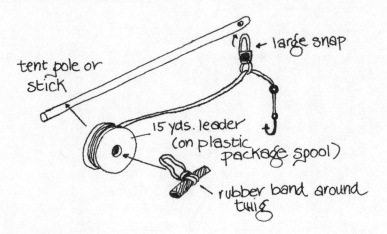

DOGGY BAG

I am one of the people who like to take their dog on a trip, and Kelly has become a premier backpacker. However, a trip with her usually meant that she wanted to sleep on (or in) *my* sleeping bag. Since she was often wet or muddy, and always dirty, it was obvious that this could not continue. So I measured her bed at home and made a sleeping bag for Kelly! It is the dimensions of her regular bed, and is made of ripstop nylon and polyester fiberfill. Top and bottom are sewn together with enough space on one side for her to get in and out easily. She either sleeps on it or in it, depending on the weather, and has not since slept on my bag. She packs it—along with her food—and it weighs about 16 ounces.

Carol Lloyd, Oakland, CA

2-3 PERSON PLASTIC TENT

This tent will resemble a lean-to with top dimensions of 6 feet by 9 feet. Use a 12-foot by 14-foot piece of builders' plastic, 8 mil. Blocked out areas are cut away. However, you may wish to leave areas "A" and "B" for extra flap protection.

No grommets are used. Instead, push marbles up under the plastic at the indicated places and tie the plastic around the marble with butcher cord, leaving a sufficient length to tie stakes or tent pegs.

String a strong line between two trees at a height of four feet above the ground. Drape the tent over the line where the top and the overhang meet. Ties are fastened to stakes. Flaps may hang or be tied out.

Draw pattern on plastic with a felt-tipped pen. Cut with a sharp knife or scissors.   *A.G. Dittmar, Morrisonville, NY*

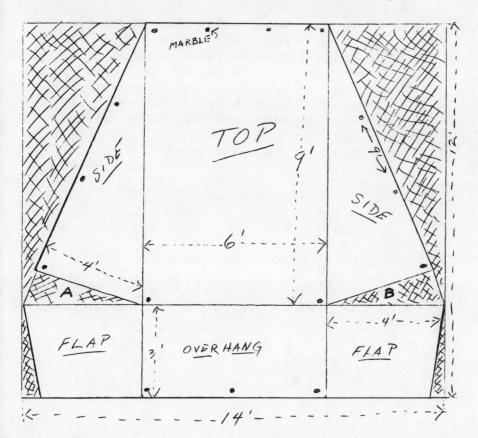

COATED NYLON TARP TENT

This idea was submitted by a lady from Pennsylvania who is an Appalachian Trail End-to-Ender. She says she started backpacking at age 49, was doing 21 miles a day with a 35-pound pack at age 53, is 61 now, still going strong and loving it! She made her tarp tent in 1970 and has been using it ever since.

The tarp tent is made of 5⅓ yards of 55-inch-wide urethane-coated nylon and a few grommets. Cost to make it now would be between $15 and $16 (compared to about $22 for a ready-made tarp tent of the same size). It weighs 1¾ pounds and is 8 by 9 feet. It is large enough for three people and their packs if packs are laid on their sides around the edges, and will easily house two people and their packs, with room to spare. Three of us slept under this in a pouring rain and stayed dry!

I use my 40-inch-long walking stick as the one pole support. It can be shifted off-center to be out of the way when three friends share the shelter. In addition to the 10 grommets around the tarp's edges, I installed 4 more to which guy lines can be fastened to pull the sides out for more height. I seldom use these, but this feature comes in handy at times. These 4 extra grommets are attached to the folds in 2- by 4-inch pieces of silver duct tape, fastened on the outside of the tarp in the manner shown.

Helen R. Arnold, Lebanon, PA

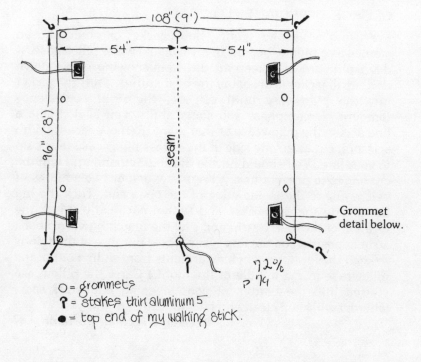

O = grommets
? = stakes thin aluminum 5
● = top end of my walking stick.

WARM WOOL PANTS

I made a pair of pants out of lightweight wool (check fabric stores for wool blends which can be machine washed, a real advantage). They are very comfortable and warm when supplemented with wind pants, and light (weigh less than a pair of jeans).

All my backpacking pants have zippers up the legs—what good will a warm pair of pants in your pack do you if it's a struggle to take off your boots to put on your pants? Make things as easy as possible.   *Dusty Linder, Union, WA*

GEORGE'S SPECIAL PILLOWCASE

For using a sweater, pants, down jacket or other unused clothes as a pillow, borrow or steal an old white pillowcase. (I dyed mine brown to keep the dirt from showing.) Your down or fiberfill jacket is probably the best stuffer. Stuff the jacket into the pillowcase until you get the right consistency (amount of plumpness and squishability you like). Make a line across the pillowcase at that point. Remove jacket. With scissors, cut away one side of the excess pillowcase fabric up to your line. You should have a big flap remaining. Hem the cut edges to prevent unraveling. Sew one or two squares of velcro pile to the inside edge of the open end. Tuck the big flap inside the pillowcase and flatten out neatly. Mark the location of the velcro strip and sew the matching velcro hook strip in position on the flap. (The whole purpose of the flap is to keep those slippery nylon garments from sliding out of the pillowcase in the middle of the night.) Carry the pillowcase stuffed into the bottom of your sleeping bag stuff sack, where it will keep clean and be handy at bedtime.

George Palmer, Portland, OR

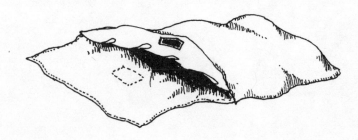

INEXPENSIVE PACK FRAME

Here is an idea for a very inexpensive pack frame that is particularly well-suited to groups (such as Scout troops) or individuals who need to keep expenses to a minimum. The frame is comfortable, weight-efficient, and cheap.

The original idea was taken from a design in *Boy's Life* some years ago. The following improvements make it a much better frame:

1. Notches in the cross bar and the cord at both ends are

the basis for a built-in jiffy diamond hitch to hold the gear package in place.

2. Roofing nails (cut off) make excellent inexpensive rivets.

3. Old car seat belts make good webbing for the bow.

For packing, all gear is wrapped in the sleeping bag (or poncho, depending on the weather), so no pack sack is needed. *J.G. Jarvis, Webster, NY*

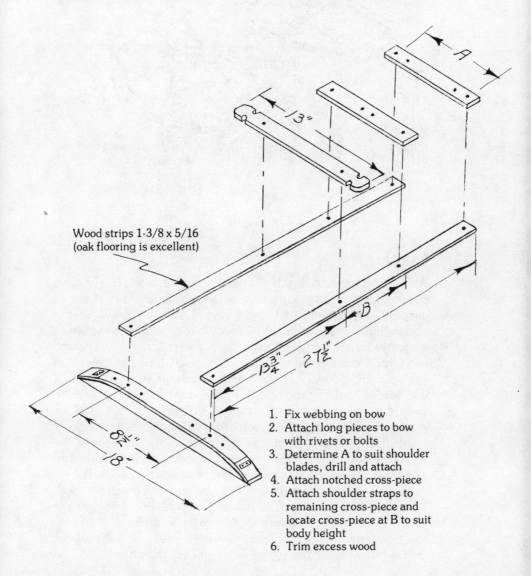

Wood strips 1-3/8 x 5/16 (oak flooring is excellent)

1. Fix webbing on bow
2. Attach long pieces to bow with rivets or bolts
3. Determine A to suit shoulder blades, drill and attach
4. Attach notched cross-piece
5. Attach shoulder straps to remaining cross-piece and locate cross-piece at B to suit body height
6. Trim excess wood

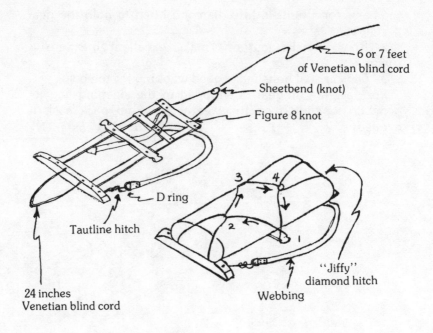

6 or 7 feet
of Venetian blind cord

Sheetbend (knot)

Figure 8 knot

D ring

Tautline hitch

3 4

2

1

"Jiffy"
diamond hitch

24 inches
Venetian blind cord

Webbing

PARACHUTE TIPI

An inexpensive, delightful shelter can be made for 2 to 6 people from a cargo parachute available in two sizes at surplus stores (about $14 and $20). Cut one or two of the panels out to make the shape more conical, and restitch the edges together partway down from the top, leaving enough room for a door opening. If you wish, sew strips of velcro on the opening edges. Let your artistic imagination run free if you enjoy color, and tie-dye the tent. Then dip it in waterproofing (such as Thompson's SportSeal or a similar product). This amount of protection will hold off a moderate rain; for more protection you can rig a plastic rain fly to the tipi with clothespins. If the tent is rigged so that its walls are at a fairly steep angle, snow and wind are deflected well.

To put up your parachute tipi, tie the top line to a high limb (or to a line strung between two trees) and secure the shroud lines at the bottom with tent stakes. Base diameter can be made smaller by increasing the pitch of the walls or larger by lowering the top and decreasing the pitch.

To use this tipi in snow, first dig out blocks of snow which you then form into a circular lower wall, over which the tipi is erected.

FIRE STARTERS

Fires, of course, should be used most judiciously (sometimes not at all). For emergencies, however, every pack should contain a few fire starters of some sort. These might be candle stubs, chunks of paraffin, fuel tabs, strips of cardboard egg carton dipped in paraffin, or one of the ideas that follow.

Fire starters can be made by cutting 2-foot sections of newspaper 2 inches wide and rolling them up. Wrap each roll with string and dip in melted paraffin (or old candle pieces). Let dry. The wax coating keeps the starters dry in wet weather and provides encouragement to a balky fire.

Tim Tackett, Russellville, AR

1. Cut newspaper.

2. Roll it up.

3. Wrap with string.

4. Dip in wax (let it soak up).

5. Let wax harden.

6. Use it! (Lights best on end.)

Put 12 briquettes into a cardboard egg carton. Over them pour a thin layer of melted candle wax or paraffin. When cool, tie the lid on. For a portable charcoal fire, light and let burn down to coals. For use as a fire starter, one or two sections of the box can be broken off.

Mrs. John H. Morton, Rochester, NY

Fill the depressions of a cardboard egg carton with melted paraffin, old candle stubs, or discarded crayons too short to use. If you wish, insert a piece of cotton wick or string in the center of each egg cup when the wax has begun to cool.

Catherine Larsen, Fox Lake, IL

BACKPACK FOR A HORSE

We recently took a 6-day trip into the Uintas Mountains on horseback, using packs we made by modifying Frostline's "Hitchhiker carryall kit #111." Cost for each kit and the extra materials required totalled about $15. The packs were very serviceable and held lots of gear. Essentially what we did was: add an extra pocket on the front, enlarge the ends to make a deeper space that rode at the horse's sides, lengthen the top straps so they could be used to lash our sleeping bags on top of the packs, add extra outside pockets to the ends, and put a series of webbing loops on the bottom for attaching tie straps to the saddle. In addition to the basic Frostline kit, we used 8 inches of velcro for pocket closures, 2 D-rings (to fasten the sleeping bag straps), a 46- by 21-inch piece of coated pack cloth to match that in the kit, and about 2 feet of 2-inch webbing for the loops in the bottom.

Pam and Ken Rislow, Salt Lake City, UT

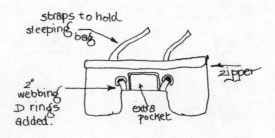

DOUBLE-DUTY SIGNALING DEVICE

Although I am not so inclined, several friends and acquaintances like to solo-backpack. In doing so, there is more thought to safety and survival in case of injury or illness. To avoid use and carrying of flares and such, a friend wanted some other sort of double-duty signaling device to pinpoint his location should people have to come and rescue. The solution was a "safety tarp." It is a regular coated nylon tarp/fly with grommets all around. It can be used as a ground cloth, rain fly, etc., with one important difference.

The tarp is forest green. The *underside* of the tarp has a large "X" sewn on it from corner to corner both directions, in fluorescent safety orange. If need be, the tarp can be hung or merely placed on the ground in a clear spot, X side up, so that location is immediately pinpointed. The bright orange X can be seen for great distances by air or ground rescue and stands out in virtually any kind of terrain, with the probable exception of the deep orange canyon walls of the Grand Canyon. Since all solo hikers make their plans, locations, whereabouts known, the rangers can easily spot the tarp's orange X within the general geographic location.

Carol Lloyd, Oakland, CA

COMBAT THE STUFFING BLUES!

A neat item is a slightly different kind of stuff bag. I got tired of cramming my sleeping bag into a just-big enough stuff bag, so I decided to remedy the problem. I now use a regular stuff bag, but I sewed up the open end, made an incision down the long length, and put in a zipper in that long opening. Now, I *gently* stuff the sleeping bag into the stuff bag and zip it closed. No more hassling a complaining sleeping bag into its too-tight stuff bag. Works great (and is probably easier on the bag)! *Carol Lloyd, Oakland, CA*

WELL-PLACED POCKETS ON A SHIRT

This idea is for those of us who enjoy making our own gear. Since shoulder straps on a pack cover a part of the pocket on the front of many shirts, added convenience and comfort can be had from making a shirt with no pockets on the front. Since I make my backpacking shirts with raglan sleeves or saddle shoulder sleeves for additional comfort and leave the pockets off the front, the shirt cloth under the shoulder straps of the pack is smooth, which greatly reduces the possibility of chafing. The question is what to do about pockets for all those items one needs often during the day. The answer: Sew the pockets on the outside of the sleeve, centered front to back, and equidistant between shoulder and elbow. For ease of sewing, the pockets should be attached with the sleeve lying flat before it is sewn together with a seam.

Just choose your favorite pocket pattern—open at the top, buttoned, flap with button, flap with velcro closing, or whatever—and you're in business. I prefer altering a pattern by making the pocket one inch narrower and one inch longer than usual. I also like a no-flap pocket closed with a button sewn on the sleeve and buttonhole on the pocket, but that's strictly personal preference. The main idea is to get the pockets out of the way of the shoulder straps, but still placed where they are usable.   *Paul L. Downey, Nashville, TN*

Be sure to check out these other suggestions that can apply to make-it-yourselfers:

4.

Recycling

From civilized to wild in 24 easy lessons! Look around your house [and place of work] for all kinds of great items which deserve another go-around. Treat them to a reincarnation in the outdoors. Here are several suggestions to get you in the use-it-again-a-new-way frame of mind.

FREE COOK KIT FOR A GROUP

Inexpensive cooking pots can be made from tin cans. For large groups, use a couple of #10's (large, institutional size cans) to cook in. For smaller groups the #5 size can (large juice cans) works well. Lids can be made from aluminum foil or another can can be placed over the top of the one being cooked in. Wire handles can be added to make lifting easier.

Kim Pingatore, Norfolk, VA

Since most of our foods use boiling water for preparation, we have developed the practice of using recycled coffee cans instead of cooking pots. Just make two holes near the top and attach a piece of wire for a bail handle and a piece of tin-foil for a lid. When they have been burned, blackened, etc. at the end of the trip, we stuff all our unburned garbage in them and drop the whole thing in the garbage can at the trailhead. Saves a lot of wear on our good pots and costs nothing.

Carol Lloyd, Oakland, CA

WATER TOTER

Cut a one-gallon square plastic jug (the kind milk or juice comes in) in half lengthwise to use in carrying water or as a washbasin. It takes no room in your pack, since it can be lashed to the outside on the pack corners.

Dorothy Blattner, Portland, OR

The one-gallon plastic jug also makes a dandy bailer for your canoe or kayak. Trim it as pictured. The squarish jug works better than a rounded one, since its sides allow you to scoop flat on the boat's bottom.

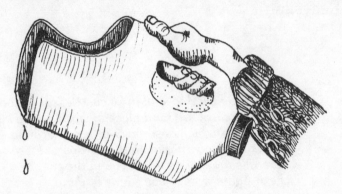

BAG YOUR BAG (AND OTHER ITEMS)

Some shoe stores and book stores give out colorful plastic bags with drawstring closures. The bags work perfectly around a sleeping bag in its stuff sack. In case of a slight shower, you don't have to get out your pack cover, and yet your most important piece of equipment is kept dry.

Margarite Hoefler, Kansas City, MO

If you can't find a free source, these bags can also be purchased at many libraries (for books) and department stores (shopping bags) for 15 to 25 cents each. They are often made of two layers of plastic, and are surprisingly sturdy, given reasonable care.

FROM KITCHEN TO TRAIL

A couple of old absorbent cotton dish towels take less space than a large, bulky bath towel, dry quickly, and are more versatile. *Happy Mulflur, Portland, OR*

PACKABLE, WATERPROOF CYLINDERS

Keep your own (or beg from friends) nifty little metal or plastic cylinders that cigars come in. They have a positive screw-on lid and are neat for carrying spare batteries, waterproof matches, fishing line and sinkers, extra clevis pins and rings, etc., etc., etc. A cylinder makes a neat container that can go into any pocket on your pack and prevents contents from getting wet. I have used them for dozens of items and find that they cannot be matched for an emergency supply of tampons (for us female packers). They also often hold my supply of rubber bands, paper clips, pencil (safely, for a change), and even my wilderness permit—it doesn't get wet!   *Carol Lloyd, Oakland, CA*

FUEL KEEPERS & FILLERS

For short trips I carry fuel for my Optimus 8R stove in discarded liquid detergent bottles. The bottles I use are those that have a pointed top which the user trims, creating a small hole allowing the soap to be squirted out. I keep tops which have not been trimmed (so that the fuel does not squirt out). But I also substitute another top which has had an opening cut for use in filling the stove. This saves carrying a funnel.

Dick Abbott, Ottawa, Ontario, Canada

QUICKIE STOVE

I call this the reusable, recycled, quickie stove. It's made from two cans: one large can like the tall juice can or the shorter one that fruit usually comes in. A smaller can (from tuna or cat food) is used underneath to hold one egg cup candle (one section of a cardboard egg carton which has been filled with melted paraffin).

Here's how: After removing the top of the empty juice can, turn it over and puncture the edge all the way around, being careful not to completely detach the top. This round of ventilation holes can also be made just below the rim, rather than on the lid, if you like (with the latter method, there's a little less blackening of the can you cook in). Melt paraffin, old candles, and crayon stubs in a double-boiled can, and pour it into a cardboard egg carton. When partially cooled and set, you can add a cotton string wick to each egg cup if you wish. This is really not necessary, since you can simply light the edge of the cup for maximum heat output instead of lighting a wick.

To cook with your stove, put one egg cup candle in the smallest can, set the tall can over this, and put whatever you want to cook on top, in a metal cup or another can. If you can find a third can for cooking, of a size that will nest between the other two when packed, it will make a compact unit that keeps all the black soot in one place. This whole stove package, with four egg cup candles, weighs less than half a pound. Each candle (when lit around its edge) burns at least 20 minutes with a *hot* flame that can boil a cup or two of water easily. If you want to forego the cost and greater weight of a stove, and are planning a very simple menu, consider making and using this cooking package.

Catherine Larsen, Fox Lake, IL

ANTI-BUG JACKET

In these parts they sell a Japanese-made raincoat which has a tightly woven nylon outer layer with a plastic coating on the inside. The coats work well for a season or two, but then the plastic coating separates from the nylon. At that point they are useless as raincoats. However, the remaining nylon shell makes an excellent light jacket to wear in fly season. Being yellow, the material is less attractive to heat-seeking bugs. The jacket is light, easily carried, and quite durable. Its hood can be drawn tight around the face. Any plastic that remains adhering to the nylon can usually be picked away by hand, but much will come away after a few trips through the washing machine. If the jacket lacks a drawstring at the waist (very useful in the fight against blackflies), then a hem is easily sewn in and a drawstring pulled through.

Dick Abbott, Ottawa, Ontario, Canada

FILM CANS VERSATILE

Empty 35mm film cannisters (obtainable free at film processing places if you don't have a supply yourself) make nifty little containers for storing both liquids and powders. They're plastic and have a snap lid that seals well.

Kim Pingatore, Norfolk, VA

Glue a round of coarse sandpaper inside the lid of a plastic 35mm film can and fill it with strike-anywhere matches, heads downward. You'll need to trim about half an inch off the matches. *Martha Andrews, Portland, OR*

If you carry different items in several film cans, label each by using an indelible felt-tipped pen.

SMALL GEAR ORGANIZERS

Putting all the necessary odds and ends in a pack can make for difficulty in locating the little ones. My wife and I, inveterate recyclers, happened on little ziplock-type bags in which myriad items now are packaged. They are ideal for carrying a few pills, a needle and thread, some waterproofed matches, all sorts of items that would otherwise fall to the bottom of the pack. They are also great in a fishing tackle box, for lures, hooks, sinkers, etc. And they can be strung together on a string and lifted out en masse for quick access.

They are totally watertight and reusable many times. Best of all, they can be found free in nearly any home, since many products are packaged in them . . . rubber bands, for instance. My source is my work—a newspaper—where border tapes come to us in bags about 3 by 3½ inches, and we use these tapes by the hundreds. Other backpackers could ask and probably get them there too.

Harry L. Elliott, Grants Pass, OR

DEADMAN HELPS IN A SNOW CAMP

I have found that the problem of pitching a tent in loosely compacted snow can be simplified by making a "deadman" out of the plastic lids that come on 5-pound coffee cans for resealing . . . the lids that look like a frisbee. Cut a small "X" in the center of the lid and pass the loop of the tent's guy line through the hole. Then use an ordinary skewer-type tent stake to pass through the loop. Pull the stake up against the plastic lid and bury the whole thing about 6 to 12 inches down, and tramp the snow down around it. It will freeze into the snow in a few minutes and is there to *stay.* I usually have to chop them out with an ice axe when it is time to take the tent down. This process usually destroys a few of the lids, so I always take half a dozen spares. And, of course, they must be packed out!

John Arrington, Poway, CA

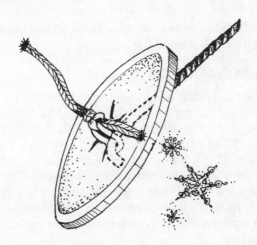

READY ACCESS PATCHES

I have found this idea very helpful for getting at my raingear easily (or other bulky items as well). Punch a hole in each end of two pieces of leather about 1½ inches wide and 4 or 5 inches long (use scraps, patches, sleeves from an old jacket, or the sweatband of a hat). Run a sturdy string through the holes and tie knots underneath so the string can't slide out. Then, sew the strips on your pack parallel to each other. Articles you want to carry handy are tied on with the string. If there isn't room on your pack for a pair of strips, even using just one is helpful.

John H. Gamble, Morgantown, WV

PHARMACY BOTTLES

Washed-out plastic bottles of various shapes and sizes can be obtained from your pharmacy and used to carry eggs, sugar, flour, coffee, etc. They are lightweight and have an excellent seal.

Jim Peterson, Bend, OR

INNER TUBE SHOCK CORDS

Shock cords for small trail tents can be made inexpensively from the inner tubes of semi-balloon type bicycle tires. (The tubes from 10-speed bikes are less satisfactory.) Cut pieces either straight across or at a slight angle to make them somewhat longer.

J.G. Jarvis, Webster, NY

NON-CRUMBLE CRACKER BOX

When I go backpacking, I usually carry a cracker and cheese lunch, but the crackers always used to crumble. Now I take the empty container that the cheese (Kraft Cracker Barrel Spreadable) came in, clean it and keep the crackers in it.

This keeps them whole and also recyclers what would otherwise be more garbage. The plastic box holds about a two days' supply for me.

Mark Miller, Westfield, NJ

 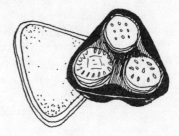

For a group, a larger version of this idea is to carry crackers and other smashables in an oatmeal box lashed on the outside of a pack. One of these round cartons holds an amazing amount of food and can be burned when empty.

SMALL SQUEEZE BOTTLES

Thoroughly wash out a small squeeze bottle such as holds Cutter's Insect Repellent lotion. Carry biodegradable hiker's soap, cooking oil, etc. These things are much costlier to purchase in tiny bottles, but you need carry only a small amount on most trips. Buy the large economy size and refill your recycled small squeeze bottle.

SAVE YOUR CHIP CANS!

Hang onto those round containers with the plastic tops that potato chips and tortilla chips now come in. They are the best ever for packing cookies, round crackers, cheese, salami, etc. and will also act as a container for a baby bottle full of powdered milk. The cans are tough and cheap and weigh practically nothing. Unsurpassed for carrying Oreo cookies! They have also been packed in such a way that they form a "brace" inside my pack, since they are quite strong and rigid. If you want, they can be burned before you pack out, since they are made of stiff paper. But I bet they will be carried out and used again and again and again. The brands in this area are Pringles and Ditto and Pinata.

Carol Lloyd, Oakland, CA

Pringles potato chip cans make fantastic organizers for small necessities. They fit just right in a pack and you can store soap, toothpaste, first aid supplies, tweezers, extra wire, utensils, and a thousand other things in them.

Ken Myers, Sherman, TX

BEDDING: INDOORS, THEN OUT

An inexpensive sleeping bag liner can be made by taking an old sheet (flat or fitted), sewing across the bottom and up the sides. The fitted sheet gives a mummy-like fit, while the flat sheet is more rectangular and roomy. A liner can also be made from a soft flannel "sheet-blanket."

Kim Pingatore, Norfolk, VA

One of the handiest items to carry in your pack is a piece of old sheet or shirt.

Washed, *ironed*, and sealed in a plastic bag, it is a sterile bandage and/or a triangular bandage.

In 1-foot squares, it is a handkerchief or pot holder.

In larger squares, it is a neckerchief or bandana.

In long wide strips it is a scarf to wear inside a wool shirt, tie a hat on, or carry wet to wipe your face on hot days.

In narrow strips it can decorate a walking stick and help you remember to pick it up, or mark a trail or other spot.

Pieces of cloth are used by peasants in Europe instead of socks — in case yours get worn out, wet or lost.

It can double as shoulder pads, padding under your rope on a rappel, or sanitary pads.

A large piece can be used as a towel, or a sarong in case you forgot your bathing suit.

I just don't wear out sheets fast enough!

R.F. Schweiker, Concord, NH

A CASE FOR YOUR WHETSTONE

Small whetstones can be carried for a while in the cardboard containers in which they are sold, but in time the container disintegrates. A substitute holster can be made from an old glove. Cut on dotted lines on both the back and palm of the glove. The whetstone slips neatly into the finger. The attached pieces from the palm and back can be tied together to secure the stone. (A similar holder can be fashioned from a small scrap of sturdy fabric such as denim.)

Dick Abbott, Ottawa, Ontario, Canada

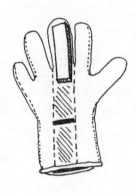

Recyclers will also want to take note of:

5.

Multi-Use Gear

To a self-propelled trekker who must travel light, the ideal piece of gear is one that has at least a dozen uses. Not many items can meet that tough standard, but here are several that try!

SALUTE THE HUMBLE GARBAGE SACK!

A large plastic garbage sack, the 30-gallon size suitable for lining your garbage can, is a most useful item to keep in your pack. It doesn't weigh much, but has a lot of uses, and it's cheap, reusable, and expendable. Its primary value is in its waterproof quality in a size and shape which will fit over most backpacks (and do a better job than the commercially made pack covers that cost several dollars, weigh more and are less waterproof). If rain or snow is a possibility overnight, slipping one of these garbage sacks over your pack may mean the difference between a soggy pack or a pack with frozen zippers the next morning, or a dry pack with all your food and clothing in good shape for the next day. When hiking in rain or snow, the plastic sack can be used to cover your sleeping bag to give it an extra measure of protection against the moisture. Perhaps with a little care you could make a few well-chosen cuts in the sack (reinforced at the ends with duct tape or adhesive tape) and slip it over your pack to protect it from the rain and snow as you hike.

The garbage sack can, of course, be used as a garbage sack. It's probably a bit large for the average backpacker's needs, but it is handy for carrying out the garbage that someone else has left behind. Not everyone has gotten the word about the wilderness ethic, and the trails into some of our most beautiful, and consequently most heavily used, areas are littered with cans, plastic containers, foil wrappers, orange peels and more. It will all stay there unless someone picks it up. The plastic garbage sack can be used to collect some of this junk and is large enough to be tied onto the outside of your pack out of your way. You don't have to fill it up, but whatever you do carry out will be appreciated by the next folks to come along the trail.

But if it's not raining, and you haven't filled your sack with other people's junk, and you come across a sloping snowfield with a nice runout, then whip out your garbage sack and get ready for a *waahoo!* Some people call it glissading, but that sounds a little too graceful for the position you're about to assume. Lay the sack on the snow, sit on it, reach down between your legs and pull one end of it up diaper-style, stick your feet up in the air, lay back, and let loose with a few *waahoos!* The plastic sack will reduce the friction between you and the snow, besides keeping your leading edge more or less dry while you make a quick trip downhill.   *Dave Kurkowski, Portland, OR*

A garbage sack can help warm cold feet at night if you slip it over the bottom end of your sleeping bag.
                                        John H. Gamble, Morgantown, WV

When you need a basin for holding water to wash yourself or clothes, dig a shallow hole (only where it will do no damage to the land), line it with a garbage bag, and fill with water. Of course, fill the hole with soil when you're through, and tamp sod on the top.   *Martha Andrews, Portland, OR*

To the myriad uses for the large garbage bag, I would add that of covering dry firewood in case of rain.

Tim Thibault, Swanton, VT

WATER BOTTLE HAS MANY ROLES

My plastic canteen (Oasis brand) is a handy item. By filling the canteen with hot water and wrapping with a shirt, it becomes a good hot water bottle. Handy for warming cold feet in a sleeping bag, but make sure the cap is on tight! This bottle is also good for placing in cold or frozen boots to thaw them quickly. This method is much preferred over trying to dry them over a stove (which may ruin them) or trying to sleep with a pair tucked away in your sleeping bag.

Michael J. Bender, Aurora, IL

SEAL IT AT HOME

The advent of home sealing machines for plastic bags has truly been a boon for the backpacker. All that repackaging of food and other items that heretofore had been in hopefully watertight containers can now be made absolutely water-proof and packaged with a flair. And important papers, too! Personal identification, club membership cards, emergency medical information, small maps . . . anything of that sort can be sealed watertight and later, unlike laminated items, the seal can be snipped after the trip and the papers put back into their original places at home. Some examples: a small map (which will now fit nicely into a shirt pocket, even in the rain), a half-dozen strike-anywhere matches, first aid supplies, toilet tissue, emergency rations . . . anything that needs extra protection from moisture can be packaged this way. The tiniest packages can be made from the scraps left over from the custom-sized bags needed for maps, recipes, etc.

Paul L. Downey, Nashville, TN

NET BAG: NO WEIGHT, MANY USES

Take along a net bag (made from nylon netting or purchased

from lingerie shops). The bag is neat for drying socks and underwear, makes drying dishes and utensils a cinch. Just fill the bag and hang it from a tree . . . the breeze does the rest. This bag is cheap, tough, and doesn't weight enough to compute.   *Carol Lloyd, Oakland, CA*

CLOTHESPINS DO IT

Carry a few spring clothespins (regular wooden ones or the smaller, plastic backpacker's clothespins) for tent-making, clothes-drying, rigging a flashlight overhead in your tent, etc.   *Happy Mulflur, Portland, OR*

PAPER CLIPS

Put a supply of paper clips in your repair kit. They make excellent bag closures, can be used as an emergency keeper ring for clevis pins, and can be used for hanging clothes out to dry securely—just bend it lengthwise and put one end in a buttonhole; put the other bent end over a line or through a line on your pack. You can bend a paper clip into the shape you need hundreds of times without breaking them. And do you know what a paper clip *weighs?*

                                    Carol Lloyd, Oakland, CA

DAY PACK HAS DOUBLE LIFE

Instead of using a stuff bag for my sleeping bag, I use a day pack. Then, when up in the mountains working out of a base camp, I have a smaller daypack along. It is also more protective than a regular stuff bag, especially since my sleeping bag travels at the bottom of my pack. Also, if you put it on the pack right, you can come up with an extra pocket or two. Either stuff the straps into the bag or use them to attach the bag to your pack.

                                    Jean Noel, Jr., Glasco, KS

STUFF SACK/DAY PACK

For a lightweight, inexpensive pack for side trips, I made one from my sleeping bag stuff sack. Buying one yard of 2-inch-wide jute braid ($1.19 per yard at fabric stores), I cut the strip in half and sewed the two 18-inch lengths onto the stuff sack, parallel and about 9 inches apart. Then I also carry a large plastic garbage bag. When I want to use the pack, my sleeping bag goes into the large garbage bag. Total additional weight is less than three ounces. This is a crude pack, but most sufficient for carrying lunch, camera, flashlight, or whatever is required for a side trip.

Diana Weir, Salt Lake City, UT

Carrying extra weight when you can make double use of what you already have is silly. Using your sleeping bag stuff sack as a day pack works great. But instead of carrying separate shoulder straps, as is sometimes suggested, I use the ones off my pack frame. This will work only if they are of simple design, attached by clevis pins at top and bottom or if they loop through U-rings at the bottom (a la Kelty). All you need do is to sew two loops of webbing to the bottom seam of the sack, at opposite sides. The straps tie into the drawcord on the stuff sack at the top. (Put one end of the cord through

the grommets in both straps and tie off. Then pull sack shut with the other end of the cord.) The lower ends of the straps loop through the web loops on the stuff sack and back up to the buckles, or tie to the loops with short pieces of cord if you have grommets on the lower ends of the shoulder straps.

You can't fill the sack very full without it turning into an uncomfortable barrel shape, but it will hold a lot of things. And you carry zero extra weight in your big pack!

Dusty Linder, Union, WA

TOUGH TRANSPARENT POUCH

The plastic zipper pouches intended to carry pencils (normally snapped into a three-ring binder) are great for packing trail snacks, eating utensils, toilet articles, navigating tools (map, compass, paper and pencil), and any other items you want to keep all together. These pouches are heavier and easier to open and close than ziplock plastic bags, yet you can always see what's in there without opening them up, which is a real convenience in camp and on the trail.

Kent Gardner, Salt Lake City, UT

CLOSED-CELL FOAM

A small piece of closed-cell foam (Ensolite) is useful to insulate your stove from the cold ground, as a sit-upon (especially welcome on snow) and to wrap crampons in before lashing them to your pack or stowing inside.

Janet Peterson, Cold Spring, NY

BRING ON THE BANDANAS

Instead of backpacking with bulky, heavy towels and washcloths, use bandanas and cloth diapers. The all-purpose bandana will serve nicely as a face cloth and the small diaper works well as a towel. Both dry quickly and can also double as potholders, nose-blowers, hats, headbands, and bandages.

Kim Pingatore, Norfolk, VA

A FEW SQUARE FEET

I carry one indispensable item when I go camping: a 2-foot-square piece of plastic sheet. Mine is from a torn "cheapo" rain poncho. This piece of plastic becomes a dry place to sit on in dew-covered grass. It is also an emergency waterproof container for camera equipment during a downpour. By covering a shallow hole, it can become a dishpan or a place to soak tired, aching feet.

Michael J. Bender, Aurora, IL

The plastic or coated nylon rectangle you use as a ground cloth at night can double as a pack cover (tuck it in between pack and frame) during a rain or snow shower on the trail. It could also provide overnight protection for your pack, when that seems more necessary than putting the ground cloth under your tent or sleeping bag.

Lorraine Kapakjian, Tenafly, NJ

LACES ALL AROUND

My husband, our two young sons and I all carry extra shoelaces—the kind that are about 48 inches long and cost just pennies a pair—some in our packs, some in our pockets. The uses for these shoelaces are many: hanging clothes, guy ropes for small tents, tying and carrying bundles of wood for the fire, emergency repairs and first aid duties, etc.

Kitty Wright, Elgin, IL

SHOCKING

An elastic shock cord with metal hooks at both ends can lash sleeping bag or camera to your pack, be a belt, or a clothesline, or lash a tarp securely over gear, packs, or the firewood supply.

GIVE A THOUGHT TO BAKING SODA

Consider the many virtues of plain old baking soda:
1. toothpaste (mix with salt)
2. acid indigestion (dissolve in water)
3. scouring powder (especially good because it deodorizes . . . also use for getting wine, fruit drink, or other leftover smells out of your plastic water jug)
4. sunburn ointment substitute (make a paste with water)
5. first aid for insect bites and poison ivy/oak (make a paste)
6. baking biscuits.

George Palmer, Portland, OR

Here are ideas from other parts of the book that deal with multi-use items:

6.

Wearing

Ideal clothing for vigorous outdoor activity needs to be lightweight, durable, versatile, and protective from cold, wet, sun and bugs. A layered system is best, with options for rolling sleeves, buttoning and buttoning neck openings. Clothes should fit smoothly without chafing or binding. If they are too tight, they'll restrict both freedom of motion and circulation. At least part of your outdoor garb should be wool, which retains most of its insulative properties even when wet.

There are many alternatives available in clothing, and one can spend a small fortune, a pittance, or something in between the two extremes to be well-clad in the wilds. The word is functional! *Surplus and second-hand stores frequently have the best choices for certain items, as well as being least expensive. Stretch your budget by making some of your own clothing, modifying things you already own or have found on a treasure hunt through a thrift store. Even a novice at the sewing machine can save several dollars by making rain pants or a poncho. How about transforming a pair of men's old wool suit pants into spiffy knickers [with braid trim or embroidery]? And a holey pair of thick wool socks makes a very serviceable pair of kid's mittens.*

GYM SHORTS PLUS POCKETS

Like many hikers, I've had problems with abrasion from shorts made out of heavy fabric, so I switched to wearing softer gym shorts. The problem with these is that they have no pockets. Solution: sew a couple of pockets on your gym shorts. I usually use some denim from a pair of old jeans. Just get a square of fabric, tuck the edges under so they won't fray, and sew it on along the sides and bottom edges of the pocket piece. Take a smaller rectangular strip of the same fabric and sew it along the top so that it overlaps the pocket. Put a button on the pocket and buttonhole on the flap (or snaps or velcro strips for closure) and you're all set!

Steve Nadel, Middleton, CN

RETIRE YOUR BELT

A belt can be very uncomfortable under a pack's waistband, but drooping pants are a drag, too! We solve this problem by tying two front belt loops together with a small piece of lightweight rope. A simple square knot never gets in the way. *Ed and Claire Weiser, Villa Park, IL*

NON-WICKING JEANS

Levis are okay for mild, dry weather, but in a rain they soak up moisture like a wick and then take forever to dry out. If a wind comes up, legs clad in soggy levis get cold! Jeans made from fabric with part synthetic content instead of all cotton are fairly tough, lighter weight, and have the advantage of drying quickly. They are also less expensive.

THE VERSATILE SWEATER

On equipment lists I seldom see "lightweight sweater," but this is one of my most useful items. It weighs 6 ounces (ladies' medium). In cold weather I wear it next to my skin, thus having that all-important layer of wool. It makes just the right warmth for wearing in the sleeping bag when it's just a little cool otherwise. In summer when the sun goes down I take off my sweaty damp T-shirt and put on the sweater—does it feel good! I wouldn't be without it, nor would I want one of those bulky, heavy 1- or 2-pound jobs—not as versatile. Several light layers of wool shirts and sweaters are warmer anyway.   *Dusty Linder, Union, WA*

MOCCASINS: EASY ON FEET AND THE LAND

Carry moccasins to wear around camp on long hikes. They rest your boot-weary feet at day's end, are easy to pull on even over swollen tootsies, and tuck into a smaller pack-space than tennis shoes (moccasins can even be folded). If the soles lose traction when worn smooth, glue on soles cut from car-mat, available at auto supply stores and discount marts. Save your camp area from the wear and tear caused by lug-soled boots.

SLIPPERS ARE GENTLE, TOO

A pair of lightweight, inexpensive in-camp shoes are foam-soled slippers with stretch fabric tops, available for less than $2 a pair from outdoor, discount and variety stores. They are suitable for dry conditions and easier on the vegetation than stiffer-soled footwear.

Jo Nims, Portland, OR

ZIPPERS TO THE RESCUE

It rains a lot here, so you wear your mountain parka on the trail. When I buckled the waist belt of my pack over the parka, it made a huge bunch of fabric in the front that was ugly and uncomfortable . . . and the belt covered up the flaps to the lower pockets, so I could not get to the things in them. Solution: open up the side seams of the jacket up to about the waist drawstring and insert zippers (tab end at the bottom) in each side. Then when wearing the pack, just unzip the zippers and pass the waist belt under the front of the jacket. Now I get into the pockets with ease and there are no more wet soggy puddles in the front of the jacket where the rainwater used to collect in the folds.

George Palmer, Portland, OR

partially zippered side seam

waist belt (buckles under the front of the coat)

TWO-IN-ONE-PANTS

I have an idea that everyone thinks is great, but they don't take the trouble to do it themselves. On my dungarees (I have the old wide-legged ones), I cut them just above the knee and installed zippers that can be separated so the legs come off and one has shorts. The hardware should come off on the legs part so it is not bothersome when hiking. I have had my short/long pants for some years, and they are invaluable—shorts and dungarees in just one unit!

Hazel Falk, New York, NY

VARIATION ON THE SHORT/LONG THEME

When I make a pair of dual-purpose short/long pants, I use velcro tape instead of zippers, and begin with a pair of jeans wide enough at the leg bottoms that they will pull on without the necessity of removing your boots. Cut the legs off 2 or 3 inches below the knees and sew velcro tape on both cut edges. The reason for cutting them below the knees is that you can then fold them up a couple of times. This keeps the dried vegetation from sticking to the tape when you are going through underbrush. In the fall and spring (my favorite times to backpack) when mornings and evenings get real cold and midday can be hot, the legs of these pants can be slipped on or off in a jiffy right over my boots. Saves packing both shorts and long pants.

Helen R. Arnold, Lebanon, PA

HAND SAVERS

A pair of old leather gloves is nice for picking up wood or adding a bit of needed warmth to your hands.

Happy Mulflur, Portland, OR

A pair of nylon glove liners weigh an ounce or less, cost between $2 and $3, and do marvelous things for keeping your hands warm. A pair of plastic gloves worn either alone or under or over other gloves also makes for warmer, drier hands. *Bill Straub, Pittsburgh, PA*

Cotton "dermal" gloves (made for wearing over medication on hands at night) can be bought at the drugstore for 79 cents a pair and will provide a nonbulky layer of warmth.

CONSIDER THE TENNIS SHOE

There are several advantages to wearing tennis shoes for hiking, backpacking, climbing, etc., rather than the larger, stiff, heavy mountain boots often seen on even gentle, smooth trails. Tennis shoes are: (1) faster, (2) more comfortable, (3) much cheaper, (4) quieter and less destructive to the soil. Speed and less fatigue (1 pound on the feet is like carrying 5 on the back—think about that) equals enjoyment and safety. I go light almost everywhere now, having broken down the psychological barriers and found no reason not to. Mountain boots are best for snow and ice and maybe continuous talus; jungle boots are still the best in bogs and swamps; but everywhere else, especially including stream crossing, drop the masochist image and go light!

Robert Burrell, Jr., Paonia, CO

DIAPER/TURBAN COOLS

A cloth diaper can be soaked in cool water, wrung out, wound around the head turban-style for a nice evaporation/ cooling effect. Wear it either by itself or in combination with other headgear.   *John Peck, Tucson, AZ*
[*sent in for him by James R. Jackson of Fayetteville, AR*]

WARM FEET AT NIGHT

If your feet tend to be cold at night, invest a few dollars ($9 or $10) in a pair of down or synthetic-filled socks. You can also make your own from a kit for about $7. They have no stiff soles or tough covering, but instead are more like fluffy, loose-fitting socks. They have several advantages over wearing socks in bed: being loose, they give your feet a chance to air a bit; your toes have room to wiggle; they don't impede circulation (tight socks, even if thick, can actually make your feet colder). These booties weigh almost nothing and stuff into a tiny wad in your clothes bag.

REPAIR NOTES

Snap a safety pin under your collar or inside a pocket to use in an emergency. I used one in the Porcupine Mountains of Michigan once for an end guide which I had broken off my fishing pole . . . caught trout, too!
                    Robert F. Thompson, Traverse City, MI

Adhesive-backed moleskin makes durable re-pairs to mittens and other clothing items with areas that get a lot of wear and friction. Apply two patches back-to-back: one under the hole and one over. This is also a good preventive measure before the fabric wears through. I doctor the inside of the thumb portion of wool mittens with these patches before the mittens have had much use.

Use extra-long rawhide shoelaces on your hiking boots, cutting off pieces if needed for pack repairs, etc. If you don't like to wear this type of lace, tuck one in your repair kit.

Randolph E. Kerr, Albany, NY

EMERGENCY RAINCOAT

A coat is sometimes cumbersome to carry when the weather is fair, but getting caught in a rain shower is unpleasant, too. A simple watertight garment that is easily carried yet provides wonderful protection when needed is an ordinary plastic trash bag (the 30-gallon size that costs about 10 cents each). Carry it in your pocket or a handy outside pocket of your pack. If overtaken by a shower, cut a slit in the bottom big enough to put your head through and slits in each side for your arms . . . pull it over your head and you have a raincoat! *D. Roscoe Nickerson, Butte, MT*

WARMTH AND BUG PROTECTION AT DAY'S END

When cleaning up after a long day on the trail, I take a bath, put on my long johns, then don rain jacket and rain pants for lounging around camp in the evening. I'm ready for bed, warm enough, and the mosquitoes can't bite through my raingear! *Dorothy Blattner, Portland, OR*

LEG WARMERS ARE LIGHTEST

When I'm traveling really light, I take a pair of bicyclist's (or dancer's) leg warmers instead of long pants for cool evenings. They are like long stockings without any feet and come way up on the thighs. And you don't even have to take off your hiking shorts to put them on!
Howard Hoffman, Vallejo, CA

What you wear is also discussed in these hints:

Part II

In the Wilds

In the Wilds

Now to the doing! At the trailhead or put-in spot, leaving roads and accoutrements of civilization behind, we purposefully set out to be self-reliant in places where this is the only honest, workable way of being part of things. The land ahead of us deserves our gentlest care, in return for the privilege of being guests and temporary residents.

Along with the equipment we wear and carry on our backs, there is that vital collection of knowledge, skills and attitudes without which the finest "hardware" is of little use. A valid feeling of confidence that we can live happily outdoors comes from studying what's there (such as conditions of weather and terrain) and how we can fit in. How to stay found . . . keep working feet happy . . . sleep comfortably . . . make a functional, low-impact camp . . . turn out a hearty meal easily . . . coexist with bugs and other critters . . . get water in dry conditions . . . enjoy being out whether it's hot or cold or wet.

And when the trip ends, it really isn't over. That bit of wilderness living is part of us now and we can draw on it again and again. Eventually, most outdoor-lovers devise ways to help them remember and preserve the times out, make them overlap the rest of life and keep it sane.

In this section you'll find ideas that are used while out.

They build on the advance preparation and planning done at home, and reap its benefits. They can help us feel at home in the wilds.

7.

En Route

The going is a large part of the joy for most wilderness people. It isn't just the means to the end [camp], but an important part of the whole experience of being out. Therefore, coming up with ideas that will make traveling go well has a lot of benefits. We see more, hear more, enjoy more when not distracted by blisters on our feet, inappropriate clothing, thirst, getting lost, constantly battling mosquitoes or the weather.

So here are many ideas having to do with staying happy and reasonably comfortable on the trail, route-finding, friendly cohabitation with flying and walking critters, obtaining water when it's scarce, survival tips, and traveling by canoe.

WORKING WITH THE WEATHER

It is surprising how simple adjustments in one's clothing can change its efficiency. When exerting yourself, unbutton your outer garments, especially your shirt collar. Removing gloves also permits radiation of excess warmth. Then when you stop or slow down, button up again to retain the required heat.   *D. Roscoe Nickerson, Butte, MT*

In hot weather, wet your wrists, neck, face, and ankles with cool water. Blood vessels are close to the surface in these areas, and cool water can reduce the temperature of the blood circulating throughout your body. Covering and uncovering your head is another efficient heat-loss regulator, since more than a third of the heat your body loses is radiated from your head.

PRE-TREAT YOUR FEET

To prevent blisters on feet, rub feet with rubbing alcohol for a week or so before a trip, as well as morning and evening on the trip. It works for us!   *Judy Lahay, San Diego, CA*

AND BE KIND TO FEET WHEN THEY'RE WORKING

At the halfway point of our hike we change socks, using a Wash-and-Dri premoistened towelette to refresh feet. This tiny packet is lightweight, easy to pack, and is worth $10 on a long, hot day! To air our morning socks, a simple safety pin is attached to a side-pocket zipper and through the socks. They can then sway in the breeze as we hike that afternoon.

Ed and Clair Weiser, Villa Park, IL

LACING FOR COMFORT

When lacing your boots, if you twist the laces around each other just before you hook into the last two or three hooks (or eyelets), you can have the ankle area laced tightly, which you want, and leave the arch area looser, which you also want.   *Paul Keller, Portland, OR*

DON'T NEGLECT YOUR NOSE

I just completed a two-month trip along the Pacific Crest Trail, so this idea is well-tested. I have a plastic triangular-shaped shield (available at athletic and outdoor stores) that attaches to the bridge of my sunglasses and protects my nose from sunburn. Much handier than the suntan lotion so many people use. It is always on me when I wear my sunglasses and I don't need to carry the extra lotion.

Simeon Ross, Smithtown, NY

HANG ON TO YOUR SPECTACLES!

If you wear glasses, use an elastic athlete's strap to keep them on, feel more secure and comfortable, especially in warm weather.   *Happy Mulflur, Portland, OR*

TEAM DRINKING

When backpacking, give your canteen to your partner and you carry his. This way when your partner gets thirsty he can dig out his canteen easily from your pack and vice-versa.
Thomas M. Minchin, Brooklyn, NY

BACKPACK WITH A BIKE BOTTLE

The water bottles used in bicycling work great for backpacking also. They are made to be used on the move. (Incidentally, they are great for drinking in the car while driving because they don't splash out.)
Margarite Hoefler, Kansas City, MO

A CASE FOR THE TRAIL

A skinny fishing rod case doubles as a walking stick.
Hugh Brock, Portland, OR

FOILED AGAIN!

I save the empty foil packages that Kool Aid, Tang, lemonade, etc. come in, and we all have our own individual drinking cups which fold up compactly and take up no room in our pockets. These can be used over and over again before they give out.   *Joan M. Dahl, Melbourne, FL*

A variation on this drinking cup idea came clear across the ocean from England, from a fellow who reads the "Long Trail News" of the Green Mountain Club.

As a drinking cup, I always take with me a flat plastic container, pocket-shaped. The one I use is of relatively thick, flexible plastic and used to be sold many years ago by outdoor outfitters. I have not seen them advertised for a very long time, nor have I met other hikers who knew about them. Probably one of the plastic cases provided with savings account passbooks would make a reasonable substitute.
John H. Lochhead, London, England

PONDER THE HUMBLE PRUNE

A prune pit in your mouth will keep your mouth moist and eliminate the dry-mouth feeling when hiking on hot days.

Kim Pingatore, Norfolk, VA

RINGSIDE DRINK

Attach a shower curtain ring (5 cents each) to your belt or belt loop and hang a small water bottle from it for easy access. This is especially helpful if you are hiking alone.

Happy Mulflur, Portland, OR

TAPPING A SMALL WATER SOURCE

Here is a way to get water late in the summer when most of the springs have started to dry up. Often when hiking you come across a bank beside the trail that is very wet and at one time had been a spring. But the water flow is now so slow that there is no free-flowing water. If you hunt around for some strips of bark and push one end into the wet bank (with the concave side up), water will start to flow down the trough and drip off the end. Then do the same thing again so that the first piece of bark trough drips into the second. You may have to do this three, four or more times to collect a large enough flow. At first the water will be muddy, but this will clear in a few minutes. *H.W. Kruger, Portland, OR*

KEEPING KIDDIES HAPPY

Hiking with a youngster can be tiring, especially if you just sling a regular baby pack on, because they pull on the shoulders. We tied the Gerry Kiddie Pack onto a decent pack frame. Much easier on the collarbone!

Baby will be happier in the pack (or almost anywhere) if he has something to chew on. Beef jerky is long-lasting and not very messy. Dried bananas are sticky but kids love 'em.

Cecelia Haugen, Eugene, OR

SAVE YOUR ENERGY WHEN YOU CAN

By stepping over fallen timber instead of stepping on it, much energy can be saved. Instead of lifting your whole weight every time you come to a log, lift only your legs. A 200-pound man lifts a ton by the time he steps on 10 logs!

D. Roscoe Nickerson, Butte, MT

A good hiker or backpacker will never step on anything he or she can step over. This will cause less worry or chance of twisting an ankle, and you won't get as tired.

Terry Elge, Aurora, NE

AVOIDING TWISTS AND SPRAINS

All hikers could learn something from a ballet dancer (besides grace). For balance and prevention of twisted ankles the dancer works on his/her "turnout." Point your foot straight ahead and notice how easy it is to "roll over." Turn your foot out, and this becomes almost impossible. Before I jump off rocks or logs, or as I start a hike on an unusually rough trail, I remind myself to turn my feet out and insure that the hike ends painlessly.

Jim Stacey, Stanton, KY

THE VALUE OF A SIMPLE STRAW

Carrying a drinking straw can be very useful. You can: fill a canteen from small falling trickles; slurp water from between gravel and rock fields (both common around melting snow in high country) and other hard-to-get-at places (even under surface algae in ponds if you are desperate). *Robert Burrell, Jr., Paonia, CO*

When backpacking in a dry area I always have with me a piece of plastic tubing about 20 inches long and ¼ inch or less in diameter. With this tube it is possible to suck up water from even the tiniest trickle on a rock. Such tubing can be purchased at a medical or scientific supply company.

John H. Lochhead, London, England

HOT WEATHER HELP

On hot summer hikes, instead of a water bottle or thermos, try putting lemonade or water in a plastic baby bottle and then freezing it. For the hike, wrap a face cloth around it and put it in a plastic bag. As you hike, the lemonade melts (but is still cold) and the condensation moistens the washcloth, which is then great for wiping your face.

J.G. Jarvis, Webster, NY

Perishable foods such as cheese and fruit can be stored next to a frozen poly bottle and preserved a bit longer. When you freeze the bottle, take care to allow for expansion of the liquid as it freezes. Leave cap off the bottle and shake up contents several times just as the cap of ice is forming at the top. This will permit upward expansion rather than having all the expansion go toward bulging the sides of the bottle.

Sue Hughes, Denver, CO

ON THE LEVEL

A small Locke-type hand level (available at Sears and similar stores) is a useful tool for judging your position on one slope relative to another. If you are climbing one mountain and can level-sight to a known (from a map) elevation on another mountain, you have determined the elevation of your position. *J.G. Jarvis, Webster, NY*

FINDING YOUR WAY BACK

An easy way to mark a temporary trail in the woods is to lean sticks against trees as you advance. Put these markers close enough together so on your return trip you can see two or more at a time. If your route takes you out of the trees into a clearing, be sure to make a definite mark at the edge of the trees so you can pick up the trail easily.

D. Roscoe Nickerson, Butte, MT

THE BIG PICTURE

Hikers might consider taking a pair of opera glasses with them. I bought a pair on sale for $2. Maybe they aren't as powerful as binoculars, but they are certainly lighter and more compact. *Allan Benford, Oshawa, Ontario, Canada*

A STAKE IS A SLUICE

For getting water that is barely flowing over rocks or branches, I always carry a 6-inch channeled tent stake, to use as a small sluice.

Steve Nadel, Middletown, CN

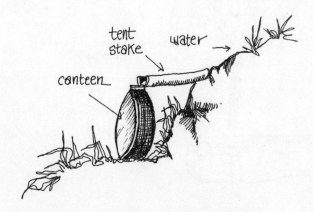

IF THERE'S A FORD IN YOUR FUTURE

When your route necessitates fording a small stream and you find yourself tossing in "stepping stones," choose the roughest, most irregular rocks you can find. When wet, these provide much surer footing than their smooth counterparts.

Nadine Cobb, Boise, ID

HELP WHEN YOU NEED IT

A police whistle on a string around the neck can be a great asset in the deep woods. Shouting may relieve your frustration, but it will not do much for getting you un-lost. Our survival class experiments showed that shouts often could not be heard over 200 yards. On whitewater canoeing trips I require all of my students to wear a whistle and, of course, we use a system of pre-arranged signals—besides the universal three blasts for "Help!" and two blasts for "Keep whistling; I'm trying to find you." As you can imagine, rapids often drown out even the shrillest yells.

Jim Stacey, Stanton, KY

DOGS AND CATTLE DON'T MIX

Nothing irks a stockraiser more than to have his cattle

disturbed, and nothing disturbs cattle more than a dog. The dog may be perfectly harmless, but cattle are suspicious of dogs and become nervous if one shows up. Avoid entering a pasture or field with a dog if cattle are present.

D. Roscoe Nickerson, Butte, MT

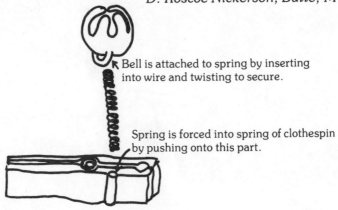

Bell is attached to spring by inserting into wire and twisting to secure.

Spring is forced into spring of clothespin by pushing onto this part.

GIVE BEARS A FAIR WARNING

For traveling in bear country last year when I explored the proposed Pacific Northwest Trail with the man who created the idea of the trail, Ron Strickland, I developed this clip-on bear bell. (A bear who has fair warning of your approach is much less likely to react aggressively . . . he doesn't like being surprised any more than you do!) It uses a spring clothespin, a large round bell, and a spring from the inside of a ballpoint pen. It attaches to the shirt of the user, or lacking clothing, it is clipped to the shoulder pad or some other place near a hand to flick the bell every once in a while.

Chris Kounkel, Spokane, WA

THE HAT SAYS SCAT!

Soak insect repellent into the brim of your hat.

Randolph E. Kerr, Albany, NY

TO SPRAY OR POUR?

The spray form of Cutter's insect repellent is nice if you're wearing long pants and sleeves. Lotion is cheaper but hard to spread over clothes (where it also helps discourage mosquitoes and flies).

Happy Mulflur, Portland, OR

ASSORTED ANTI-BUG IDEAS

Forget your insect repellent and the bugs driving you nuts! Look around for yarrow and pick it, then rub over your

exposed skin. Yarrow grows over most of North America and is safe to use.

Tom Hopkins, Arras, British Columbia, Canada

I have just returned from the wilderness of Alaska after spending two glorious months up there, and I have several useful hints that help. Of course there are no ticks as such in Alaska, but in Tennessee we make up for Alaska and all the other states in the Union. I found that buying regular dog flea and tick collars and clasping them around your ankles keeps ticks, fleas, chiggers and whatever off while hiking, camping, etc. Also, using lemon juice with a dab of salt is a natural repellent for your skin. Also I've learned that lowering your sugar intake will cause less bug bites. And . . . anyone traveling to Alaska ought to make sure they buy plenty of mosquito coils to burn.

Ron Story, Charlotte, TN

If you don't like the standard impregnated plastic flea collars, you might try the "natural" ones available at some natural food stores. They are light, tightly woven rope lengths saturated with beeswax and oils of pennyroyal and eucalyptus.

IF ALL ELSE FAILS

When bitten by a mosquito, make a wagon-wheel with your fingernail at the center of the bite to stop the itching. Make sure to depress your nail deeply.   *Jon Carey, Dexter, MI*

This idea I stumbled on by accident while taking medication to control the itching that went with an ellergy. I discovered that while taking just one or two pills daily of the yellow Chlor-Trimeton (available without prescription), neither chiggers nor poison ivy caused as much itching as they did when I wasn't taking it. This remedy does not treat the condition, only the itching that makes it so uncomfortable, and it might not work for everyone as well as it has for me.

Margaret Scruggs, Gainesville, FL

GETTING OUT OF A JAM

Sometimes in the course of your travels you may be temporarily lost. Here are a few "survival" ideas to ease the situation.

Jim Stacey has been teaching survival and outdoor skills for several years. He says:

The best survival student I ever had was a not-yet-sophisticated twelve-year-old who was not afraid to appear "silly." He stuffed every dry leaf he could find between his

outer clothes and his underwear. He looked like a scarecrow dressed in down, but he so thoroughly enjoyed three chilly nights in the North Carolina mountains that he asked if he couldn't stay another night. Adults could not do better than to observe that even in Arctic conditions our built-in heaters will generally suffice, provided we insulated ourselves properly.

Insulation and shelter materials may not be readily available in some cases and we are then forced to look to the "external heater," the open fire. But let's make the open fire a closed fire. Scrape or dig a body-sized hole (all resemblance to a grave is purely coincidental) about 6 to 12 inches deep. Build a fire therein; when a bed of coals covers the bottom of this hole, then cover the coals with *dry* dirt, lie down, and snore away. Besides offering very little usable heat, the open fire can be quite dangerous, especially to exhausted folks. I have had several students burn not only their clothes but their hair as well, as they sleepily edged closer and closer to a fire.   *Jim Stacey, Stanton, KY*

We carry a small lightweight fishing net in our survival kit. It is easier to catch fish with a net than a hook and line, when the fish aren't biting and you're trying to stay alive.
                                        Judy Lahay, San Diego, CA

PADDLE YOUR OWN . . . .

A few ideas came from canoeing enthusiasts:

Copper clad the end of spruce canoe paddles to keep them from "brooming."   *Randolph E. Kerr, Albany, NY*

Be sure to enclose any map or guide for your canoe trip in the ever-useful ziplock plastic bags. Make certain that the information you require is showing through and taped down into place on the bow breastplate for the convenience of the bowman's navigation.   *Thomas M. Minchin, Brooklyn, NY*

I am a canoeing enthusiast, but I have always had the misfortune of spilling foods while preparing meals on trips.

With no table in the backwoods it is sometimes difficult to find a flat surface. However, I recently came across a new idea for making a table in the wilderness while canoeing. You simply carry your canoe up to the cooking area and turn it upside down. Supporting it on one side with a stick or rock, you can easily make a level surface with plenty of room for your food. It's good to know I no longer have to spill food, especially when it is so vital in the wilderness.

Judy Green, Cambridge, Ontario, Canada

A canoe can also serve as a windbreak for your campfire when turned on its side.

When portaging my canoe, my arms get very tired always holding them in the up position holding the thwart (especially with a full pack also). So I hinged a 30 inch length of metal extrusion (a wooden dowel will work) to the forward thwart. A short cross-piece is attached to that. Now it's much more comfortable for my arms. When paddling, the free end of the extrusion is tied to the center thwart, helping to keep gear in the canoe. *Ed Chevalier, Sidney, IL*

canoes not having 3 thwarts could attach it to the cross-member of the front seat.

hinged

Many other ideas have potential benefits for your on-the-trail times. Please see:

8.

Camp Techniques

Presented here are miscellaneous hints for use in your camp. They range broadly over many aspects, such as caching food to protect it from bears and other four-legged friends, building a fire, waiting out a storm, making your camp comfortable and functional.

The best camp is one that disappears after you leave it! A prime responsibility of every wilderness lover is to preserve what it is he came to enjoy, leaving no marks of his passing through. This means making camp in the places that can most easily bear the burden of temporary human habitation [not the fragile meadow or the lake shore, for instance]. If you are journeying in a much-used area where campsites with fire circles and already-bare ground exist, use those places. Gather up every bit of litter you bring in, as well as what you find on arrival. Keep water sources clean by carrying water well away for washing, toothbrushing, cleaning dishes . . . and use biodegradable hiker's soap. Be very conscientious in the disposal of body wastes, remembering that the zone for biodegrading is 6 to 8 inches below the soil's surface and that pollutants can be carried many yards by rain water through soil and into a water supply. [See Verl Underwood's words of ancient wisdom on page 144.]

STAYING HAPPY IN THE RAIN

We have been learning something every time we go out. Each trip is a little more comfortable, a little easier, a little better in some way. The Fourth of July weekend was rainy in western Washington. We took a hike up the south fork of the Skokomish and camped in the woods near the first alpine meadow. We had the shelter of big trees and plenty of downed wood for a small fire. The next day we took a day hike up over Sundown Pass to Sundown Lake. Everyone we met was on his way home, having gotten wet and miserable that night out in the open at the lake where it rained and blew. And we were cozy and comfortable! We learned something about where to camp when the weather is bad—you can still enjoy your trip. A tarp is great when weather is nice or you have to travel light, but a cozy tent makes all the difference in the rain, fog and cold wind.

Dusty Linder, Union, WA

CANDLE POWER

When a candle lantern isn't enough, I use a small can with the lid still attached. I bend the lid straight up and then place a candle in the can. The lid acts as a windbreak for the flame when the candle is placed just outside my tent.

Mike Westby, Portland, OR

SAFE KIDS IN CAMP

If there are small children in your group, don't pitch camp or plan a picnic near some dangerous spot (such as a cliff or water pit). You'll be constantly running after the child, trying to keep him/her from hurting himself. Camp a ways away and enjoy the scenic spot on a hike.

Cecelia Haugen, Eugene, OR

THE LUXURY OF RUNNING WATER

For camping when water is available, take along a half-gallon or one-quart plastic milk or orange juice bottle. Punch a small hole in the bottom and insert a toothpick or whittle a twig to fit the hole. Presto! You have running water to wash hands or brush teeth with. With the twig in, loose the cap a little to let out the air pressure or remove the twig and tighten down the cap. All you have to do is squeeze the bottle, providing a fast or slow flow of water. Hang from a limb, with a towel handy if you like. *Tim Shield, Russell, PA*

MOTHBALLS DISCOURAGE CRITTERS

Back in the 1920s my uncle had a family of skunks take up residence under the front porch. He sent a letter to Washington, D.C. and they advised him to put mothballs under the porch. It worked! The skunks left! Mothballs also discourage raccoons, squirrels, mice, pack rats, and even bears . . . all these animals have an intense dislike for the aroma of mothballs. Scatter the mothballs around your camp (you can sew a few into little net bags if you like), and the critters should leave your food alone. I have camped out for a week with mothballs around camp and had no food thefts. Mothballs are effective for at least a week.

Robert McCutcheon, Mt. Holly, NJ

HOT WATER THE EASY WAY

Here is a backpacker's version of a solar water heater that I've used for two years. In a sunny area where some digging can be tolerated (not an alpine meadow, mind you), scoop out a hole 20 inches square and about 5 inches deep. Lay your sleeping pad (closed-cell preferred) in the bottom. Place a piece of 4 mil black plastic, 4 feet square, in the hole so as to form a shallow pan. Pour in 5 gallons of water. Cover all with clear plastic and seal all edges with dirt. On an 80-degree day don't be surprised if the water gets above 125 degrees, the skin's limit for most of us.

Jim Stacey, Stanton, KY

BLOW THE BUGS AWAY

Choosing a campsite sheltered from strong winds but visited by gentle breezes will discourage mosquitoes from hanging around.

BLISS IN BUG COUNTRY

I'd like to introduce my method of dealing with the ubiquitous New England insects which "grace" our woods and mountains during summer months. A lightweight and nonbulky army surplus or other bed and cot type mosquito net (used in the tropics, etc.) makes an ideal, easy to rig nighttime "bug shelter." Two adjacent trees (or firmly anchored sticks) can provide the needed support, and a tarp can be rigged over it if rain threatens. On warm nights one can experience good air circulation, and when clear skies prevail, you can enjoy the ever-popular "stars overhead" effect. Tucking the netting under the edge of a pad or air mattress assures that a person will have a bug-free night.

While on the trail, the netting can be draped over one or two people, keeping out uninvited lunch or snacktime guests. During the height of the black-fly season, my netting saved the *skin* of an incapacitated hiker who had a long wait for transportation.   *Bruce O. Brown, Quincy, MA*

CACHE AS CACHE CAN

To hoist goodies out of reach in bear country, try this easy method. Use two lengths of nylon rope: one with a small aluminum pulley on the end for throwing and hoisting your food bag/packs, with the other cord to minimize friction.

Howard Hoffman, Vallejo, CA

HANG IT ALL!

One way to keep ground-dwelling critters out of your pack is to tie it to a tree. It's easier for you to get things out of it, too. The cord you used to fasten your sleeping bag to the frame is good for this purpose. Run the cord through the cross bars of the frame and tie it tight.   *Tim Tackett, Russellville, AR*

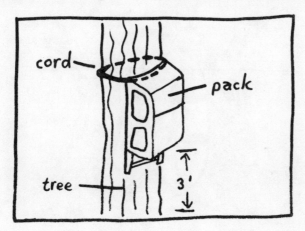

BAG A ROCK, FOIL A BEAR

One of the satisfactions of backpacking is meeting the challenge of some of its attendant frustrations or petty annoyances, such as tying a rope around a rock, throwing it over a limb for the purpose of hoisting up one's food sack, only to have the rock fall out and leave the end of the rope hanging in the tree. I made a drawstring bag of nylon net, of a size to hold a suitable rock. This is tied to the end of my rope when I find the right rock to put in it. On the other end of the rope is the snaphook which attaches to my food bag (I use the "Cache and Carry" bag by Trailhead Wilderness Supply). The nylon net weighs nothing, a rock is usually to be found wherever one is camping, and if my aim is any good it works on the first try, as long as I remember to hold on to the other end!   *Betty O'Keefe, Orinda, CA*

A PANTRY IN THE WOODS

If there are any clumps of trees handy to your campsite that have crotches, with several trunks growing out, set up small pantry-like shelves by placing flat stones in between the trunks. Be careful not to force the stones too hard or some bark may peel off. And be sure to dismantle your "cupboard" before you move on down the trail!

Tim Shield, Russell, PA

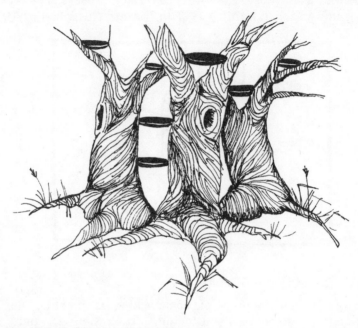

WAITING OUT A STORM?

A tiny deck of cards is fun when a group hikes together. Some other aids to confinement: pocket cribbage board, magnetic chess set, word games using only a few lettered dice, and whittling (downed wood only, please!), saving the shavings for fire starters.

SANITATION THEN AND NOW

My contribution is the instructions in the Old Testament on how to dig a latrine away from the campsite. Those old Hebrews thought of everything!

"The toilet area shall be outside the camp. Each man must have a spade as part of his equipment; after every bowel movement he must dig a hole with the spade and cover the excrement." Deuteronomy 23: 12-13, *The Living Bible*.   *Verl A. Underwood, Fort Worth, TX*

DRY WOOD STORAGE

I find that when I go camping and use a tarp slung over a rope stretched between two trees, there is wasted space where the tarp meets the ground on both sides. This place serves very well to store dry wood in case of rain.

Ken Frazier, Woodhaven, NY

HELP KIT FOR A GROUP

In a prominent place in your camp, hang this collection of items to be used in repairs, emergencies, and unscheduled chores. It can all be contained in a cloth bag about 5 inches in diameter and 10 inches long, tied with a leather thong or shoelace.

10 roofing nails; 6 20d nails; 10 10d nails; marbles and butcher twine (25 feet) for making emergency ties; 6 feet of 18-gauge copper or iron wire (to attach loose shoe soles and other repairs); 3 feet of leather thong; pliers; 3 candles; matches in a plastic bag; aspirin; bandaids; several 4-inch squares of roofing felt paper (for emergency fire starters). *A.G. Dittmar, Morrisonville, NY*

THINK BIG!

When a magnifying glass is needed (for splinter removal or treating small wounds, etc.), use the one on your compass base plate or look through the wrong end of your binoculars, held *very* close to the object (an inch or less away!). The view-finders of some cameras will also serve this purpose.

FIRE IT UP

I have never seen this idea in any book on backpacking or camping, but it works. I used it for six weeks on the Appalachian Trail, so it has been field-tested. Buy two (they'll last a month) 10-cent wax candles no more than 5 inches long . . . available at outdoor stores; not the "drip-less" dinner candles from other stores. Put them in a side pocket of your pack. When you want to start a fire for dinner, collect a small pile of tinder, nothing larger than pencil-sized. Get out your candle and light it. When it begins to burn well, turn it on its side or point it down so the candle wax drips onto the tinder. When several pieces of tinder are covered with wax, put the candle into the tinder and light it. Each piece acts as a candle wick and will burn for a few minutes, allowing you to add bigger sticks and get things going. This method is especially useful when there has been a recent rain. Remember that wood for cooking should be no bigger around than your thumb, since you need coals for heat rather than flames.   *Ed Shields, Richland Center, WI*

I was on a Sierra Club trip in the Superstition Wilderness of Arizona in March 1976 when the trip leader, John Peck, used a piece of hollow plastic tubing to stoke wood cooking fires. As sections of a cooking fire begin to die down and you have numerous pots balanced on a grate which would be cumbersome to remove, rebuild or redistribute the fire, and then replace, you put the tubing in your mouth, direct the other end to the area of the flagging fire and blow. That produces a stream of air to the part of the fire that has died down, which rejuvenates that spot so you obtain more even heating under the pots . . . without a juggling act.

James Jackson, Fayetteville, AR

Sticks or blocks of paraffin are great for starting a fire on a wet day.   *Randolph E. Kerr, Albany, NY*

Carry a plastic drinking straw in your pack to use in getting a fire going . . . delivers air to the right area and minimizes smoke in the eyes!   *E.C. Paulsen, Bennington, VT*

Make a device for blowing up a quick fire, sometimes called a ''fire tickler.'' It is made from about 2 feet of small pliable plastic or rubber tubing (from a medical supply house or drugstore) and about 3 inches of metal tubing worked into or over the pliable tubing and flattened somewhat at the outside end. The tube acts as a bellows and directs all air that you blow through it directly on a coal or two, causing it to burst into flames quickly.

Margaret K. Scruggs, Gainesville, FL

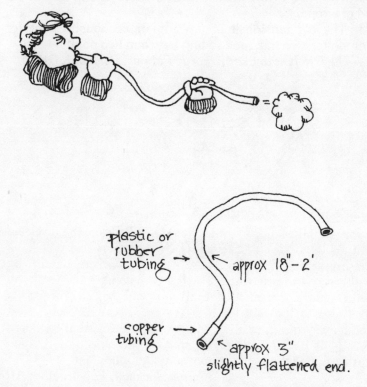

plastic or rubber tubing →

← approx 18"-2'

copper tubing →

← approx 3" slightly flattened end.

Lint makes an excellent fire-starter. (You can probably find some in the deep reaches of your pockets, the folds of your parka or sleeping bag.)   *Jon Carey, Dexter, MI*

A little "fire ribbon" in a small pill container beats a candle to start a fire. A disposable cigarette lighter is great, too, as a blowtorch fire starter (except in temperatures below freezing, where butane is inefficient).

Robert F. Thompson, Traverse City, MI

Don't build fires under overhanging rocks. I've seen 50-pound blocks fall right into the fire as the water in the rocks turned to steam and they "exploded."

Jim Stacey, Stanton, KY

THREE KNOTS YOU GOTTA KNOW

1. The old square knot
2. The old bowline (makes an undo-able no-slip loop in the end of a rope)
3. The old tension knot (an adjustable nonslip knot for keeping tension in a rope strung between two points)

The Old Knotmaker [George Palmer, Portland, OR]

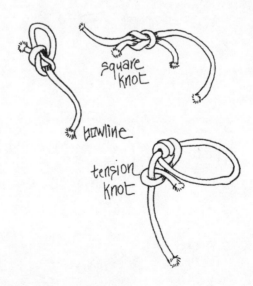

Some additional suggestions for in-camp use are:

9.

Houses and Beds

When you bought a sleeping bag and basic shelter, you made choices by applying a number of criteria such as: size, cost, weight, sturdiness of construction, design, and primary place and season of use. Using those same criteria, sift through the following hints on houses and beds to find those that will fit your own particular situation. Consider when and where you camp, whether you usually travel alone or with others, what kind of weather you must adapt to, and what are your comfort requirements for a restful night in the wilds.

BUG-PROOF TARP

If you want to take a tarp on the trail because of the savings in both cost and maintenance as well as the lighter weight, but wish to have some protection from insects, try a tarp with this modification. Purchase mosquito netting about 3½ feet wide and the length of all four sides of your tarp. Cut to fit each side, hem the edges of the netting to prevent fraying, and sew to the sides of the tarp. You will have a shelter that can be erected any way you want and still stop the mosquitoes from buzzing in your ears at night. (If you may be using your tarp at times when there's no insect problem, perhaps you'd want to use short strips of velcro on tarp and netting instead so they can be separated.)

Skip Harris, Pennsauken, NJ

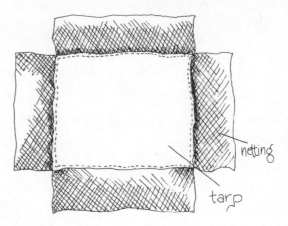

HAVE A BALL!

I realize the use of plastic (polyethylene) sheeting as a tent fly is by no means a new idea. However, when used as a fly for some tents, there is a tendency for the tops of the tent poles to poke through the sheeting. I use practice golf balls (the lightweight ones with many holes in them) slipped over the ends of the poles. The same kind of balls can also be used to secure guy lines to plastic sheeting flies. I carry a few guy lines already prepared with slip knots, ready to push over the golf ball and pull tight. Of course, the purist would prefer to use round pebbles found on the tent site—but what do you do in the Canadian Rockies where most pebbles have jagged edges?

Dick Abbott, Ottawa, Ontario, Canada

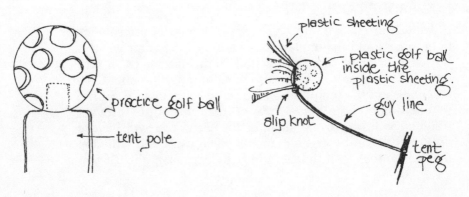

EMERGENCY ON-THE-TRAIL RAIN SHELTER

A group hiking in rainy territory should carry an 8- by 12-foot sheet of thin-gauge plastic, about a dozen marbles and butcher cord ties several feet long to attach at intervals along all four corners. This emergency shelter rolls into a small packet and should be placed in the pack where it can be available at a moment's notice. When a sudden downpour comes, all scurry together under small trees, spread the plastic, and everyone gets underneath and busies himself attaching the ties to small branches. This is accomplished in a jiffy and all stay dry. We've done it on several occasions, and it has saved the day!   *A.G. Dittmar, Morrisonville, NY*

PROLONG YOUR TENT'S LIFE

A ground cloth does much more than provide moisture protection! A good way to save that beautiful piece of nylon called a tent (which probably cost you close to, if not more than, $100) from a lot of wear and tear is to carry with you a piece of plastic tarp the same size as, or a little larger than, your tent floor. In essence, this ground cloth keeps the bottom of your tent cleaner and less prone to ripping. It also keeps that one sharp stick or rock that you missed from showing up in the middle of the night. The ground cloth weighs just an ounce or two, takes up little room in your pack, and makes additional insulation between you and the damp, cold ground. Considering its cost of less than $1, it's a sound investment many times over, for it will add years to the life of your tent.

Peter Garver, York, PA

HOUSECLEANING TOOLS

Keeping your tent dry and free of abrasive dirt inside will make it last longer. Carry a weightless, small plastic sponge (pennies at the variety store) packed with the tent for mopping up puddles from condensation, tracked-in snow, etc. If your travels are in the woods or sandy country, you might also want to carry a small travel whisk broom (about 50 cents).

LONG LIVE THE TUBE TENT!

You can establish a ridge-line area on your tube tent by placing four strips of black electrician's tape on the tent as shown. This will insure that all of the minute puctures will be on one area . . . the bottom. If you do not do this and rotate the tent, you will have myriad holes that rain loves to find and penetrate. I suggest you do this before your first use of the tent.

C.L. Gardner, Pleasanton, CA

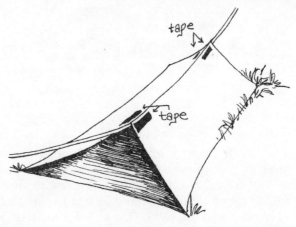

BUG-PROOF YOUR TUBE TENT

Want to discourage flying insects from sharing your tube tent? Try a piece of fine-meshed nylon net at each end, fastened with small camper's clothespins to the tent and rope and tucked under the end at the bottom. You can put together this bug-proof, rain-proof, lightweight shelter for less than $5! *Lori Rasmussen, Portland, OR*

PROBLEMS WITH SMALL TENTS

As I do a lot of hiking alone, I have thought it best to buy a very small nylon tent. Its front opening can't be much more than 30 inches wide and 30 inches high. It isn't easy to get into the tent, especially if one uses the single vertical pole supplied with the tent. To make it easier to slide into a very small tent, try these two modifications:

Improvise an A-type support in place of the single vertical pole. I use two poles of ordinary length from a standard two-man tent. To secure the upper ends of the poles, one pole slips into the grommet which would otherwise be used for the single vertical pole. The other pole's upper end slips into a bowline knot tied in the extreme upper end of the front guy line.

Even using the A-type pole arrangement described above, it still isn't easy to slide into a small tent. I put a small sheet of plastic outside the door, sit on it, slide into the tent, and pull the plastic in after me. (I do this because if it is left outside and it rains, it is no fun to slide out in the morning onto the puddle of rainwater retained on the top of the plastic!) *Dick Abbott, Ottawa, Ontario, Canada*

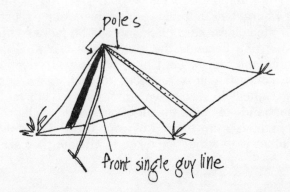

poles

front single guy line

TWO PADS + ONE BAG = COMFORT

Having a sleeping bag with a foam bottom makes a lot of sense, since your body weight is compressing any down under you and it isn't doing any good. Why pay the price of down to put under you? You have to carry an insulating pad anyway. A full-length foam pad with a down- or synthetic-filled top weighs the same as or less than a down or synthetic bag plus a separate pad (even a short one). We use this system: two 2-inch-thick open-celled foam pads which zip together and are covered with a barrel-shaped bag opened flat and zipped around the perimeter of the pads. This combination is actually lighter (although bulkier) than the two bags and two short pads we carried before . . . and are the thick pads comfortable!   *Dusty Linder, Union, WA*

NO CREVASSE RESCUE NEEDED

Friendly sleepers who use a double bag can make two air mattresses into a double one. With a kit available at fabric stores, make three pairs of eyelets along one side of each mattress and lace the two together at night with short shoelaces. No chasm caused by the mattresses separating!

DO YOUR ZIPPERS GET ALONG?

If traveling with a warm friend, be sure your sleeping bags are compatible for zipping together . . . one right- and one left-handed!   *Eleanor Adelman, Portland, OR*

ASSORTED SUGGESTIONS TO INSURE A WARM SNOOZE

Warm up *before* you go to bed, and hop in the sack quickly! Put your morning clothes inside your sleeping bag down at the foot where they'll provide added insulation between your legs and the cold ground (dressing will be more comfortable in the morning because the clothes are warm). Pile extra gear under the foot of your bag, where your sleeping pad doesn't reach. If you wear socks to bed, make sure they aren't so tight as to slow down circulation in your feet. Keep a knit hat handy to don if the night gets really chilly . . . a lot of heat escapes from the top of your head! Don't wear the same clothes to bed that you hiked in all day; they are bound to be a little damp, and will chill you. Since your body gives off moisture even during sleep, air your sleeping bag each morning if possible, to rid it of dampness which would make you cold the next night.

A NATURAL HOT WATER BOTTLE

When I was a little girl in South Dakota I lived with my grandmother. It was very cold in the winter and our 14-room house was heated by wood stoves. On the back of the stove in the kitchen sat large rocks. Yes, each of us had a rock; all day it stored heat, and in the evening when we retired we got our own rock, wrapped it first in a newspaper and then a towel, and cradled it closely while we trudged up a staircase to our cold bedrooms. The rocks never burned through the paper, but they kept us warm all night. Backpackers could use this idea if they placed rocks in their campfire when the mountain air plunges down the old thermometer. (Caution: don't use river rocks which can contain moisture, causing the rocks to explode when heated!)

Marcia House, Portland, OR

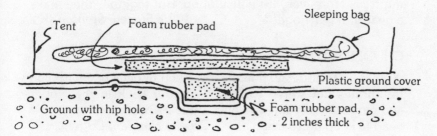

Tent   Foam rubber pad   Sleeping bag

Plastic ground cover

Ground with hip hole   Foam rubber pad, 2 inches thick

AN IMPROVED HIP HOLE

Here is a way to sleep on the hard ground and be as comfortable as if in your own bed at home. As you know, a hip hole dug in the ground helps a lot, but I have found a way to make the hip hole even better. I dig the hole approximately 1½ inches deep and 10 inches in diameter. The sides of the hole should be tapered to remove the sharp edge. Then take a 2-inch-thick piece of foam rubber 10 inches in diameter and place it in the hip hole after laying your plastic ground cloth over the hole. After these are in place, pitch the tent, and then put down your sleeping pad and sleeping bag. The best place to carry the small foam pad is in your stuff sack with your sleeping bag. (Please use this idea only where digging is appropriate and will not injure the land. And of course, refill the hole when you move on.)

H.W. Kruger, Portland, OR

Stuff bag

Foam rubber

Sleeping bag

TREAT YOUR TENDER BODY TENDERLY

If you're big (like me) but tender (like me), at least when it comes to sleeping, the best combination of comfort and insulation without too much weight that I've tried is: a piece of Volarafoam (close-celled foam) on *top* of a short, individual tube air mattress such as Air Lift or Hampshire makes. The close-celled foam offers almost no padding; the mattress offers very little insulation. But together they make a beautiful marriage! *Jim Stacey, Stanton, KY*

CUDDLE WITH A KID

A child up to about 40 pounds can sleep in your bag with you (mummies not suited to this). Put your back to the zipper and curl around your wee one. I put a knit cap on my son's head to keep him warm. *Cecelia Haugen, Eugene, OR*

$1.50 FOR AN AIR MATTRESS

Use about 4 or 5 feet of plastic air bubble packing material (24-inch width costs 30 cents or less per foot). It is lightweight and folds up into a fairly small roll. Available in many art departments (it is sold for mailing paintings, etc.).

Dianne Wright, Lake Oswego, OR

A SOFT, QUIET PILLOW

Many of us use our clothes bag as a pillow. If you don't like the feel or sound of the coated nylon or plastic stuff sack your clothes ride in, sew a small pillowcase (with end closure of snaps, lightweight zipper or velcro) from soft sheeting or lightweight flannel. At night, fill the case with your jacket or other extra clothes and lay your weary head down in quiet comfort. If your trekking is done in dry circumstances, this pillowcase can be your only stuff sack for clothes.

A VERSATILE BAG FOR YOUR BAG

A year or two ago I decided it was wasteful to carry a ground cover *if* I made something better. The result was a sleeping bag cover or bivouac bag which is waterproof nylon on the bottom, ripstop nylon on the top, with a zipper down one side. These fabrics keep pitch, moisture, etc. off your expensive sleeping bag and provide a built-in ground cloth. However, I went one step further and made the top piece a double layer with ¼ inch of fiberfill sandwiched in between. The fiberfill top adds several degrees of warmth and cannot absorb water. On very warm nights, I sleep in the cover alone or on top of my sleeping bag but under the top cover. Just enough warmth to be comfortable and to foil the bugs. Your sleeping bag can be inserted inside the cover or simply laid on top of it.   *Carol Lloyd, Oakland, CA*

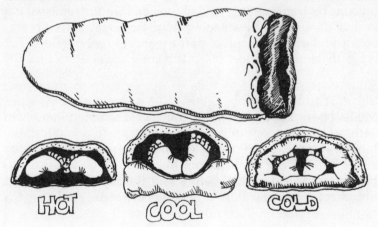

HOT   COOL   COLD

ADD A LAYER OF WARMTH

You can improve the warmth of a synthetic-filled sleeping bag (without buying down) by making a lightweight but warm comforter for it. Get two sheets of nylon coated with a film of Dacron II (used in making jackets) and sew it together . . . sort of a loose bag within your sleeping bag. Should keep you warmer than down, because down is worthless when wet.   *Judy Lahay, San Diego, CA*

A BAG FOR ALL SEASONS

I have a Gore-Tex bivouac bag that gives excellent service and has many advantages. (This breathable, waterproof laminate is available by the yard for about $8.25, and in ready-made items such as my bag.) Your sleeping bag stays cleaner when used in this cover. The bivouac bag's added insulation turns a summer bag into a three-season bag and a three-season one into a winter bag. If you travel by yourself, there is no sense carrying a bulky tent that could weigh up to 7 pounds, when you could carry a 1-pound bivouac sack. It will probably stuff into the same sack that holds your sleeping bag. On a hot night you can be protected from insects if you sleep on top of your sleeping bag, but under or inside the bivouac bag. My Gore-Tex bag has a hood which can be pulled over during rain for protection. Even if you are sleeping inside a tent, enclosing your sleeping bag in a bivouac bag will prevent spilled food and water from soaking in and damaging the sleeping bag. Because of its breathability and good waterproof performance, I feel the Gore-Tex is worth its higher price!   *Woodie Krugel, Portland, OR*

GO SOAK YOUR FEET

My feet get cold, and climbing into a cold sleeping bag, even with socks on, never quite got my feet up to a comfortable temperature . . . and good sleep never came. Now after the supper dishes are washed I put the pot back on the fire and heat up some water. Just before I hit the sack I stick my feet into that lovely hot water!   *Peggy Hohmann, Andover, CN*

SWEET DREAMS!

Place shoes or boots under the head of your sleeping bag to form a slightly raised pillow. (You can increase comfort by topping this irregular lump with a layer of clothes, such as your jacket.)   *Randolph E. Kerr, Albany, NY*

When pondering shelters and sleeping systems, consider also these helpful ideas:

10.

Fixing and Feasting

*Ah, the joys of a fine meal prepared with ease in
the wilds! And what a drag when cooking and eating
don't go well! Like a good night's sleep, good eating
adds immeasurably to the success of a wilderness
venture. Here are some suggestions to help things
go smoothly in the culinary department. Combined
with the at-home preparation ideas presented earlier
in the book [Chapter 2], they will add ease and
pleasure to your wilderness feasting.*

GET IT TOGETHER

In a small stuff sack or ziplock plastic bag, carry several
general cooking items that are used from meal to meal, such
as: matches, biodegradable liquid soap, several sheets of
paper toweling, a nylon net scrubber or something else that
will do the job (how about half a Tuffy or Chore Girl?), army
can opener, cleaning needle for your stove burner.

MULTI-USE FOIL PANS

Buy those little round aluminum foil baking cups (about 59
cents for 10 at a variety or grocery store). They are super for

including in your cook kit. Use them for setting up Sierra Salad or other gelatin desserts, puddings, stewed fruits, applesauce, fruit cocktail . . . on and on. You have a perfect-sized container that will "prepare" the food and serve it. They are easily washed and dried, weigh about ½ ounce for four of them, and can be used indefinitely. I mix the food in a ziplock bag and pour it into the little pans to "set." Four (or more) neat little servings. A bonus is that you can also bake in them either at home or on the trail, warm something up in them, or heat water in them. They also serve well as an emergency or extra drinking cup.

Carol Lloyd, Oakland, CA

SHELTER FOR YOUR STOVE

I occasionally need to construct a windbreak for my stove. I carry stove, fuel, etc. in a wide shallow stuff bag. The bag spread out, with a stake in each side (inside) properly located, makes such a windbreak. Sometimes one of the tent stakes and the shock cord holding my sleeping bag to the pack have to be utilized as additional support. One can afford to carry a little larger bag for stove and related equipment if you convince yourself it is also a windbreak. Wet the bag if you are worried about burning it.

Jean Noel, Jr., Glasco, KS

PINT-SIZED PAN

The pint-sized aluminum canteen cup (now made in Japan from the G.I. pattern) makes a good second pan for two people. It's the right size for heating water for a hot drink, with a piece of foil for a lid. It fits in an army canteen or inside your larger pot. I carry it and a 2-quart pot and sometimes a frypan . . . and have never needed more. My frypan is a teflon pie plate with the rim bent up in one spot to accommodate a pot-grabber.   *Dusty Linder, Union, WA*

SQUARING OFF

A square-bottomed spoon (trim a wooden one yourself if you can't find one this shape) gets into corners of your pans more efficiently than the standard rounded shape.
George Palmer, Portland, OR

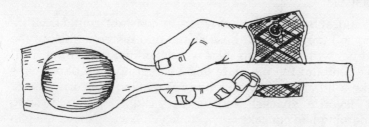

TOSS AND TASTE

A frisbee can do double duty as a plate. (And you can also slide down a snowfield on it!)
Kent Gardner, Salt Lake City, UT

TRAVELING STRAINER

A large nylon net square doubles as a strainer for noodles or spaghetti and as a pot scrubber. It is weightless and compact.   *Eleanor Adelman, Portland, OR*

DISCOVER MESSLESS COOKING

One idea that we have used in our Explorer post to ease the drudgery of pot cleaning is the use of bake bags. These are the type of plastic bags you can buy in the grocery store (about 10 cents each) for baking roasts, turkeys, etc. We use a lot of grocery store foods such as Tuna Helper. We place all the ingredients (including the amount of water called for in the directions) into a bake bag (the regular size, for meats up to six pounds, is useful). Then, by placing the full bag (closed loosely with the wire twist fastener provided) into a cook pot which has one to two cups of water in it, it is possible to cook the ingredients in the bag. The pot remains clean and the bag can be burned or packed out.

Bob Joseph, Poughkeepsie, NY

Willard Reed of Northville, NY, who also uses the above messless cooking method, notes that the hot water in the pan can be used to clean eating utensils.

COOL IT!

A pot-grabber will get hot when in constant contact with a pan, so I carry a small hose clamp and fasten a stick to the grabber with the clamp (nice when working over a hot fire). An aluminum foil pie plate and two spring-type paper clips make a lid. This rig works fine for making popcorn (one of our favorite snacks) and is very light. When cooking something like pancakes on a stove you have to move the pan around constantly or the pancake will burn. (I'm stuck with a husband who doesn't think he's camping unless he has pancakes for breakfast!)   *Dusty Linder, Union, WA*

WHO FORGOT THE SPOONS?

This idea proved a life-saver for my brother and me while camping upstate on a three-day hike. At our first meal we discovered neither of us had spoons or forks. We knew from past experience that eating with a pocket knife was dangerous and not worth the risk of being cut. Then an idea hit me. Chopsticks! We found some slender *dead* branches, broke them into about 8-inch pieces, and stripped them of their bark. Ahah! Chopsticks! They provided us with a new outdoor experience. No weight to carry around, as we could burn them after meals. Not to mention an exercise in finger dexterity. We could stab, mix and pick up food, and we did. That weekend was a good one.

Garry D. Maynard, Wapp Falls, NY

DEVOUR YOUR DISH!

On a summer weekend trip when food weight isn't crucial and fun is, take cantaloupe and instant cereal (oatmeal, Zoom, etc.) for breakfast. Eat the melon half first, then use it as a bowl to blend cereal and hot water.

TURN YOUR HIKING STOVE INTO AN OVEN

One way to make an oven on the trail without using an open fire: Start with an 8-quart aluminum pot and lid. Inside this pot, place a couple of metal tent stakes to make a rack. The pan you put the food in should fit inside the 8-quart pot with about 1 inch of space around the sides. Put the lid on the big pot tightly and put on the stove, using a low flame. This can be done on a smaller scale, as well. Forks, handles, spoons will also work on the bottom as the rack.

Tim Tackett, Russellville, AR

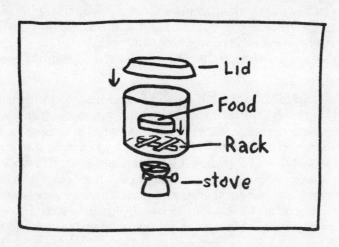

DON'T LOSE YOUR BURNER PLATE

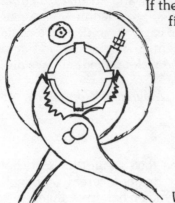

If the burner plate on your Svea stove fits rather loosely on the burner head, make this simple adjustment to avoid the worry of losing it. Such a loss renders the stove almost useless. My two-minute solution: Use a pair of pliers or a similar tool and bend the four ears holding the plate to burner head in toward the center of the stove.

William M. Byram, Arcanum, OH

PRIME TIME

To prime a gasoline stove which has no pump (such as Optimus or Svea): Remove the fuel tank filler cap, open valve, blow into the gas tank, watching the nozzle opening. When sufficient gas has collected in the priming cup at the base of the stem, stop blowing into the tank, close the valve, replace the filler cap, and light the fuel.

Bill Straub, Pittsburgh, PA

Instead of using fuel from your stove's tank for priming (which blackens the stove in the burning), carry a lighter fluid can that has been emptied and refilled with methyl hydrate. Perfectly clean, smells pleasant even if it spills, and lights your stove without creating a black coating (which then gets all over the contents of your pack).

Murray Cleland, Flesherton, Ontario, Canada

Here's an idea I got from a good friend (Richard Furman of Huntington NY). Preheating of white gas stoves can sometimes be a problem, especially in winter. To help solve this trouble, cut up the cover of cardboard egg cartons into strips ½ inch wide and 2 inches long. Melt some paraffin in a tin can which is set in a pan of water (for safety). Using tweezers, simply dip the strips into the melted wax, remove and let cool on newspaper. I usually make about 50 or 75 strips at a time. Store as many as needed in a plastic bag along with your stove. This cardboard seems the best, as it is porous and soaks up a lot of wax.

To use, wrap one strip around the stem of your stove. Light the strip and let burn until the flame is almost out, then open the burner valve. If enough pressure has been created, a loud blue flame will appear. If not, quickly add a second strip to the still-burning strip.

The Optimus mini-pump has made use of this technique unnecessary. But for those who can't use the pump on their stove or do not want to buy the pump, this idea is second best.   *Gregory Horne, Truro, Nova Scotia, Canada*

A butane lighter doesn't work in the cold, as we found out last week on a ski tour on Mt. Rainier; a regular refillable lighter would seem better.   *Dusty Linder, Union, WA*

THEY GROW ON TREES

Goatsbeard lichen makes a good pot scrubber!
            Marilyn Anderson, Portland, OR

FOIL WINDSHIELD

A piece of heavy-duty aluminum foil can be used around your stove as a windshield and heat reflector. Be careful not to totally enclose the stove in a shield that is too close to it, however. The fuel tank could overheat and explode.
            Margarite Hoefler, Kansas City, MO

A COMPLETE SMALL COOK KIT

My lightweight Optimus 99 stove is about 5 inches square and has a lid which doubles as a small cooking pot (holds 2 cups of something simmering or heats 3 cups of water if you have a very steady hand). On trips when my food plans are a little more elaborate, I carry the stove in a 1½-quart lightweight aluminum saucepan which I bought for less than $2 and "squared off" a bit to accommodate the square contours of the stove. I also removed the handle from the pan. The addition of this larger pan to my cook kit broadens cooking possibilities, is ample for two people, and increased the weight by only 3½ ounces. The total package is about 6 inches square and 5 inches deep.

THE VERSATILE BABY BOTTLE

Buy and use the two basic sizes of plastic baby bottles on the market (about 65 cents each, 4 or 8 ounces). They are a neat shape, have ounce markings graduated on the sides, and are leakproof. They are super for mixing dry milk and similar liquids and can be suspended in the cold stream by a loop around the neck of the bottle. Just remove the nipple and glue the two-part lid together for a leakproof seal. The tops screw on, and a bottle will fit in a pocket of your parka or pack. You can also leave the nipple on and use as a milk squirter. Very lightweight and cheaper than most hikers' water bottles. Being made for babies, they are nearly indestructible! *Carol Lloyd, Oakland, CA*

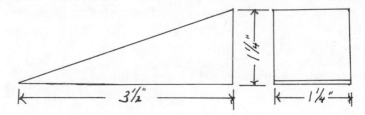

ON THE LEVEL?

I carry four simple wooden wedges to use for instantly leveling my gasoline stove when I find the cooking surface is not quite level. One or two are usually sufficient.

Esmond Milsner, San Francisco, CA

LIKE BAKED GOODIES ON THE TRAIL?

This is an adaptation of a commercial ring-shaped oven for use with a backpacker's stove that is marketed by Optimus for about $15. A recent magazine article described a homemade adaptation of this on-the-trail baking apparatus, and I have made a modification to improve its performance. Use two 1½-quart ring molds (the kind you use for molded salads), one nested inside the other to reduce the risk of burning your cake. Cut the outside wall down to within 1 inch from the bottom, as the upper area doesn't seem to burn (saves a little weight). For the lid I use a teflon-coated frypan (which I take mainly for making pancakes and

·omelets), with the handle removed. I bent the rounded lip on the mold to support the frypan. All the gaps and holes make for good ventilation, which also helps avoid burning. The homemade oven is lighter than the commercial one (6 ounces vs. 15 ounces). This doesn't count the weight of the frypan lid, since it has other uses. The lid on the commercial oven serves only this one function.

Robert W. Love, Whitmore Lake, MI

He and two friends spent a week on Isle Royale Wilderness Area in Lake Superior and made cakes every day with this arrangement!

LIGHT, CHEAP REFLECTOR OVEN

To bake biscuits, take your messkit frying pan, make a half-dome hood out of foil to reflect campfire heat. Add some margarine or oil, biscuits, and place facing fire. Keep flames built up right in front of pan. If coals build up, you can cook the bottom side at the same time by resting the pan on coals. Split the biscuits and pour hot fruit compote over them . . . mmmm! *Janet Peterson, Cold Spring, NY*

STRIKE ANYWHERE? WHERE?

When starting my stove with "strike anywhere" matches (which I have previously dipped in melted paraffin for waterproofing), I sometimes have difficulty finding a place to strike them. To get around this problem, I glued a strip of very coarse sandpaper to a handle of the pot grippers. These are always available to me when starting the stove, as I keep the stove, nesting pots and pot grippers in the same bag.

Robert Peterson, Binghamton, NY

SPEED BREAKFAST UP

If stewed dried fruits are on the breakfast menu, start soaking the fruit in water to cover the night before (either in a ziplock bag or the pan they'll cook in). In the morning they'll be rehydrated enough to need only a few minutes simmering . . . thus saving time and fuel.

CLEAN WATER AID

We use a portable charcoal water purifier called "H2OK." It cleans and purifies the water so boiling is not needed. Can also be used at home, and weighs only a few pounds. The weight would preclude using this idea in most traveling-light situations, but a group might find it useful for areas where they *know* purifying large quantities of water will be necessary. *Judy Lahay, San Diego, CA*

SUSPENSE

A 2- to 4-foot length of lightweight chain can serve as a handy system for suspending pots over a campfire (combined with a straight stick held horizontally over the fire in forked branches). Wire small hooks onto both ends of the chain so the height of the pot above your fire can be adjusted. This method is most useful with pots you've made from cans and fitted with wire bails. The chain won't burn and it stows nicely in a very small space.

Paul Keller, Portland, OR

While fixing and feasting, you might also find these hints useful:

11.

Living with Cold and Snow

An increasing number of outdoor enthusiasts are discovering the special joys of winter trekking and camping. There is quiet and solitude rarely found these days by the summer adventurer [unless he goes off the trails.]. A simple, exquisite beauty overlays the land, and there is delight in discovering a familiar place in its winter dress.

Probably one of the strongest appeals of being out in winter is that these conditions call for all the competence and resourcefulness one can muster, for the margin for error is slim. The consequences of being poorly equipped in gear or knowledge can be tragic.

The winter traveler must first have experience and knowhow in getting along outdoors under less severe conditions. Then he must learn how to work with the special problems of cold and snow: cold injuries; increased caloric needs; route-finding without the aid of trails, signs and blazes; putting up a shelter when tent stakes won't hold; keeping body and gear warm and serviceable; getting along with little or no liquid water.

The rewards of successfully and happily meeting the challenges of cold and snow are many: a satisfying new level of wilderness competence, the extension of outdoor activities to include the whole year, the freedom to enjoy new places in new conditions.

TOGGLES ARE TOPS!

If the stuff sacks you use in winter have just drawstrings which require knots, buy spring toggles (about 35 cents each) to streamline closures. Toggle can be worked with just two fingers, even cold ones.

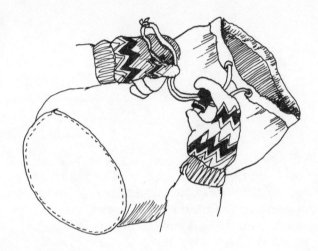

FREE FINGERS

Use hunter's mitts with a slit in the right palm for cross-country skiing. Fingers can be freed easily to adjust ski bindings, etc.   *Randolph E. Kerr, Albany, NY*

ZIPPER PULLS

For cold-weather packing, make 3- or 4-inch shoelace loops on all pack zipper tabs . . . easier to manipulate with be-numbed or mittened fingers!

KEEP YOUR ZIPPERS ZIPPY!

During snow-camping season, occasionally treat zippers on your pack, tent, and parka with a silicone lubricating stick available in variety, auto parts, or hardware stores. This will help them work more smoothly and shed the moisture that can lead to freezing up.

STABLE TABLE FOR STOVE

If you experience a problem of locating a suitable position for the safe use of your stove, use a snowshoe placed firmly in the snow along with a piece of ensolite pad to protect your snowshoe and carefully cook an enjoyable winter dish.

Thomas M. Minchin, Brooklyn, NY

WARM, DRY HANDS IN THE KITCHEN

With my snow-camping gear I carry a large pair of lightweight latex or plastic gloves to wear when cleaning pans and eating utensils (using either warm water or snow). The gloves are large enough to wear over a pair of wool gloves. My hands stay warmer than if I "did the dishes" bare-handed, and wool gloves stay dry. Sheer vinyl gloves cost as little as 50 cents a pair, and heavier latex ones are only $1 more. *Kathy Tollefson, Beaverton, OR*

Lacking plastic gloves, use plastic produce or bread bags over your mittens to keep them dry.

Also wear plastic gloves over wool ones when pitching and taking down your tent (often a wet, cold job). This will encourage you to brush off all the snow and icy condensation that you'd otherwise be packing with the tent.

WARMING DRINKS

Heated juices are tasty in nippy weather. Try V-8 juice, with bouillon added to taste. Also . . . spice up hot fruit gelatin drink with flavored brandy.

Thomas M. Minchin, Brooklyn, NY

NIGHTTIME NIBBLES

Keep a nighttime food supply handy by your sleeping bag for times when you wake up cold. High-carbohydrate foods such as fruit, candy, crackers will boost your body temperature a bit. (This hint assumes you're not in bear country, where all food should be hung away from the sleeping area and *none* kept in the tent.)

WARM DIGITS

Carry two hand warmers with you when winter camping. That way you will always have a safety device for your hands during the day, and you can slip one in each of your boots at night, keeping the boots warm and dry for the next day's activities.

Thomas M. Minchin, Brooklyn, NY

SNOW CAVE LIGHT

Make a niche in the wall of your snow cave to hold a candle set in a sierra cup. Votive candles are short and stable and fairly long-burning.

COLD WEATHER CLEAN-UP

To clean your pots during freezing weather, fill them with water. After it freezes (usually overnight), chip out the ice or heat it up a bit so it slides out. Your pot will be clean.

Mike Westby, Portland, OR

A FREEZE-FREE WHISTLE

Many hiking books recommend that people carry whistles with them on the trail. I always do, but mine is plastic instead of metal . . . much more comfortable to use in very cold weather! Most signal whistles marketed are made of metal, but in our north country, hockey referees' whistles are plastic.   *Allan Benfore, Oshawa, Ontario, Canada*

You could also wrap adhesive tape around a metal whistle.

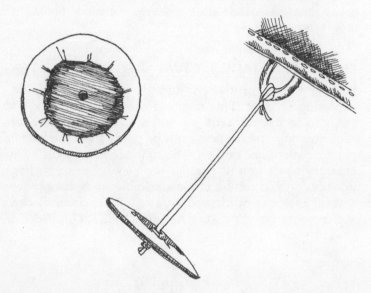

SNOW PEGS FROM CAN LIDS

Snow pegs are heavy and expensive (up to $1.75 each). Instead, take the top and bottom from a tin can (soup size), cover the edges with tape so you won't cut yourself, and drill a small hole in the center. To use, take a short piece of utility cord, put one end through the hole and knot it. Tie the other end of the cord to the peg loop on your tent, stretch taut and bury the lid in the snow. Voila! A snow peg. It makes a very effective deadman in snow or sand, is lightweight, and eight or ten of them stack very easily into a small ditty bag.

Howard L. Lasky, Gaithersburg, MD

TREAT THOSE FEET WELL!

Wearing rubber boot socks when skiing and snow camping not only keeps your feet dry, but also adds a layer of warmth and eliminates the hassle of frozen boots in the morning. These pullover socks are worn *over* your boots in wet snow conditions. They cost about $4 a pair. Buy them large enough so you won't be stretching them too much when putting them on, because that's what causes rips in the rubber. If tears do develop, the boots can be repaired with silver duct tape. (Remember? You have some wound on your pack frame.) If you ski in pin bindings these rubber boot socks can be used after poking matched holes in the tape-reinforced soles.

MORE HOMEMADE SNOW STAKES FOR YOUR TENT

I prefer to put up my tent and leave it in place while I go exploring on skis. This means I can't use my skis and ski poles to secure my tent guy lines. Lightweight anchors for securing guy lines in snow can be made from the bottoms of plastic gallon-size bottles. The tops are mostly cut away but enough is left to pull against the snow. These anchors are lightweight and can be made stackable (to reduce bulk) with careful choice of bottle and/or a few judiciously placed cuts at the sides.   *Dick Abbott, Ottawa, Ontario, Canada*

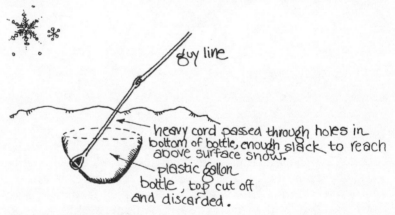

guy line

heavy cord passed through holes in bottom of bottle, enough slack to reach above surface snow.

plastic gallon bottle, top cut off and discarded.

TAPE STORAGE WHEN SKIING

Several feet of silver duct tape is a great thing to have along for repairs of many kinds (overboots, tent, gaiters, parka, pack, stuff sack, etc.). When you're skiing, the perfect place for storing the tape is on your ski poles! Always accessible and takes no room in your pack. Having tape on your poles makes it available even on day trips or forays out of a base camp, when your tape-equipped pack (see page 17) is not with you.

DON'T LOSE YOUR LENS CAP!

I recently completed a 68-day traverse of Mount McKinley here in Alaska and took innumerable photographs. One thing that made cold weather camera work considerably easier was a simple string device to secure the camera lens cap so that it wasn't lost in the snow or dropped from mittened hands. A short length of fishing line is attached to the camera body or case and a small hole is pierced or drilled in the lens cap's center. The line is run through the hole in the cap and knotted or heated to prevent its slipping out. The photographer merely pops the cap off to shoot and lets it dangle on the line until it's replaced. It is out of his way and leaves hands free to manipulate controls or hold the camera snugly. This modification is both convenient and practical. Best of all, it can be easily done by anyone in approximately 15 minutes time.   *Jack Duggan, Anchorage, AK*

SHOVEL AND DEAL

A lightweight but reasonably sturdy snow shovel can be made for $2 to $3 from either a piece of sheet aluminum or a cookie sheet (about 12 inches wide and 16 to 18 inches long). Cut a hand-hole near one end and shape the lengthwise edges to form a bevelled fence about ¾ inches wide. With a file, smooth off any rough edges that might snag your other gear.

This 9-ounce, almost-flat shovel will pack easily and has many uses around a snow camp besides its obvious role in building snow caves, igloos or trenches. It can be a windbreak for your stove, a shelf for the candle that lights your snow cave, platform for a small fire (carry in a plastic bag after it gets sooty), and even a hanging card table for your tent! The latter use sure beats playing four-handed rummy on lumpy sleeping bags during those *long* winter evenings!

To turn your shovel into a card table, punch a hole near each corner with a large nail and file down the rough edges. Cut four pieces of string about 4 feet long and tie a bulky knot in one end of each. When threaded through the holes, these knots will support the "table" and the other ends will be attached at the top of your tent's ceiling. Many winter tents are igloo- or tipi-shaped and have clothesline loops overhead. If your tent has no convenient place to attach the table's "legs," you might want to add a loop yourself.

BARGAIN BRITCHES THAT DO THE JOB

Old downhill ski pants, *as long as they're loose enough,* make great cross-country ski wear. Cut off the stirrups that run under your insteps, since they can cause chafing. The fabric sheds snow and rain well and usually insulates enough so that long underwear is not needed. Check your local thrift shops for these bargains at $1 to $5 a pair! Or turn medium- to heavy-weight wool pants into knickers by cutting off below the knee, sewing on a cuff with velcro or button closure.

FOOT WARMERS FROM FOAM

To increase the insulative value of your boots, cut out a pair of insoles from thin closed-cell foam. It is available in ¼-inch thickness as well as thicker. Be sure the insoles you add don't make your boots so tight that circulation is impaired, or you'll be working at cross purposes.

STRONG LIGHT BELOW FREEZING

A lithium-cell flashlight works better in sub-freezing temperatures than one with standard or even alkaline cells. It is considerably more expensive, but maintains a much stronger light output and has a shelf life of several years.

KEEP YOUR HOUSE SNUG

Whether or not your tent has "snow flaps," pile a few inches of snow around the outside at the edge of the floor; keeps cold wind from blowing under the tent floor and chilling the occupants.

Snow-trekkers will want to check out these ideas from other sections of the book; they can add to your winter pleasures:

12.

To Help You Remember

The memories of our wild times are treasures to preserve and savor again and again. Each has his own special way of keeping these experiences clear and alive in memory. Some take pictures, write, paint, collect things. Others have no tangible reminders of their treks, but prefer to rely on memory alone and use the time while out for simply being there. Most of us need a little help, however, especially as we spend more and more time in the wilds and expand our horizons to dozens of places. Here are a few suggestions that may trigger a special way for you to save your wilderness ventures.

COLLECT A COLLAGE

One summer my kids and I collected a small piece or two of downed wood (mostly no larger than 2 by 4 inches) on every hike . . . something with an unusual shape, color or texture. We assembled these into a collage glued on a stiff background and set this in a natural wood frame. This reminder of a treasured summer now hangs in the living room and is a part of our daily lives.

185

SIERRA CUP SCRAPBOOK

My sierra cup took on an added special value to me when I began etching inside the bottom the names of mountains I've climbed.

PLANTS INTO PRINTS

On a climb to the summit of gentle Strawberry Mountain in central Oregon, I gathered one sample of each of the grasses and flowers that grew there. I pressed and dried these and later made prints on rice paper, mounted on cork blocks for friends' Christmas gifts. The water-based block printing ink was gently rolled onto the sturdier plants, and the fragile ones were carefully laid on a puddle of ink. Then each was used to print its image on the rice paper, in a pleasing, balanced grouping.

SUMMIT ART

So you'd like some proof that you did reach the top of the mountain? Take along in your pack a little rubbing paper and a piece of rubbing crayon. Make a rubbing of the benchmark at the top and start an attractive collection.

J.G. Jarvis, Webster, NY

ANIMAL AUTOGRAPHS

Making plaster casts of animal tracks is easy on the land and gives you unique, long-lasting reminders of where you've explored. One dollar buys 1½ pounds of Plaster of Paris powder, enough for *many* casts and certainly more than you'd want to pack on any one trip. Carry the powder in a ziplock bag (*label* . . . it looks just like instant pudding mix but isn't nearly as digestible!), then simply add water and mix in the bag when casting (2/3 cup powder mixed with 1/3 cup water will make a cast 3 to 4 inches in diameter). Carry a cardboard strip about 2 by 10 inches for each cast you make, plus a paper clip for joining the ends to form a fence around the track. Quickly pour the Plaster of Paris (mixed to buttermilk thickness) into this fence. Work fast! The plaster begins to harden almost immediately. Wait about 30 minutes for it to set.

WILDERNESS NOTES

I like to keep a small notebook and pencil in my pack which I use to keep a log of each of my backpacking trips. The more times I go out, the less clear the details of any one trip become. So toward the end of the trip or when I've returned home and am cleaning out my pack, I make a few notes about the trip I've just been on. The dates, where we went, who was in the group, and any other item which is worth remembering, such as the especially good or bad weather, the hordes of mosquitoes, or uncommon wildlife or plant life spotted along the trail. I know that all these things are locked into my memory and that a short note is the key to bringing them out. And remembering my past backpacking trips is the next best thing to planning my next one.

Dave Kurkoski, Portland, OR

FEATHER SAFE

Take an envelope for safely carrying feathers you find in the woods (probably the lighest, least bulky kind of collection for remembering trips).

WHERE HAVE YOU BEEN?

If you hike with a walking stick, use a burning tool or a hand grinder to note on the stick the places it has taken you. It's a nice reminder of good hikes in lots of interesting places.

J.G. Jarvis, Webster, NY

Suggested Books on Backpacking Basics

Ground-level information on equipment and techniques can be found in these excellent books. They are the ones I recommend to students in beginning backpacking classes, as aids to developing both skills and attitudes for outdoor adventuring.

Backpacking: One Step at a Time, by Harvey Manning (Vintage Books Edition, Random House, NY 1973).

A delightfully realistic and readable guide, charmingly illustrated. Sound help for the awed beginner and an indispensable reminder/expander for the seasoned traveler.

Pleasure Packing [How to Backpack in Comfort], by Robert S. Wood (Condor Books, San Francisco 1972).

A well-written book that aims to "take some of the work out of wilderness backpacking so the beauty and happiness are free to shine through." The chapter on food is more thorough than most, and there are sections on family trips and on trout fishing.

Walking Softly in the Wilderness, by John Hart (Sierra Club Books, San Francisco, 1977).

This comprehensive volume stresses low-impact wilderness methods . . . how to enjoy and be part of the land without abusing its vulnerability. Direct, sensible, well-organized, and full of helpful bits of information that will stay with you and affect the way you live with the wilderness. Good illustrations with a purpose.

The Joy of Camping, by Richard W. Langer (Penguin Books, Inc., Baltimore, 1974).

"The Complete Four-Seasons, Five-Senses Practical Guide to Enjoying the Great Outdoors (Without Destroying It)." In addition to treating all the basics of equipment and techniques, also speaks of canoeing, kayaking, winter travel, weather, wildlife, nature photography.

Joy of Backpacking [*People's Guide to the Wilderness*], by Dennis Look (Jalmar Press, Inc., Sacramento, 1976).

Joyful person-to-person talk on simplifying, improvising, creatively approaching the challenges and pleasures of the wilds. Combats the trend toward elitism that has grown with technology. Much "people talk" conveys a variety of experiences and ways to go.

Notes on What and Where

Many ideas in this book mention products by brand name or name companies where items can be obtained. Although no endorsement is intended, we usually retained the use of a product name because it is a clearer descriptor. Often the mention is self-explanatory, but readers may appreciate having the addresses of three firms cited by contributors:

Frostline Kits (mail order plus several retail outlets)
Frostline Circle
Denver, Colorado 80241

Natural Food Backpack Dinners
P.O. Box 532
Corvallis, Oregon 97330

Trailhead Wilderness Supply
P.O. Box 19019
Oakland, California 94619

K-Kote is a seam-sealant available at most outdoor stores at a cost of about $1 for a tube of 2 fluid ounces, with an applicator tip. It is used to waterproof the seams of parkas, packs, tarps, tents, and similar items.

Velcro tape is used for closures on pockets, cuffs, tent flaps and many other places where it substitutes for a zipper. It consists of a pair of nylon tapes (one with hooks and one with pile) that lock together under slight pressure but may be pulled apart. Velcro comes in various colors, is usually an inch wide and costs about $1.20 per yard (for *each* part of the pair).

WOULD YOU LIKE TO SHARE?

You have probably hit on many fine, creative ideas in the course of your own wilderness adventuring. If you would like to share some of them for a possible future edition of this book, we'd be delighted to hear from you! Just send your ideas, with a sketch if it helps explain things, to:

June Fleming
Victoria House
P.O. Box 12552
Portland, OR 97212

INDEX

Hanging items from your pack, 26-27

Horsepack, 84

I

Ice desserts, 56

Identifying your gear, techniques for, 24

Insect repellent, 130

J

Jacket, anti-bug, 93

Jeans, non-wicking, 110

K

Knife, keeping sharp, 31

Knots, 148

L

Lace, how to repair, 39

Leg warmers, 117

Lens cap, securing, 181

Level, hand, for navigation, 128

Leveling stove, 170

Lichen, goatsbeard, 169

Line, shoelaces as, 106

M

Maps, care of, 39, 40-41

carrying, 41

streamline, 40

Magnifying glass substitutes, 146

Marking temporary trail, 128

Match containers, film can, 93

Match striker, 171

Meat, fresh, how to carry, 53, 59

Meat loaf, meatless, recipe, 60

Meat rolls, with cream cheese, 53

Medicine, packing, 33

Melon/bowl, 167

Menu planning, 56

Messless cooking, 165

Monster boots, homemade, 73

Muesli, breakfast, 49

N

Natural Foods Backpack Dinners, 60

Net bag, 102

Nighttime food supply, 178

Nose protection, 124

Notebooks, use of, 187

O

Opera glasses, 128

Organizers, ziplock bag, 93

Oven, homemade, 72, 170

reflector, homemade, 171

stove converted to, 167

P

Pack

attachments, 26

attaching to, 95

cover, 106

cover, garbage sack as, 99

frame, homemade, 80

legs for standing, 25

organizing: medication reminder, 33

non-skid loading, 25

reflective safety strips, 24

rope for handling ease, 29

webbing shoulder-strap washer, 30

Pack strap pocket, 38

Pad, sitting, 105

Pants, lightweight wool, 79

short/long, 112

ski, modified, 182

Paper clips, uses, 103

W

Z